MAKE EACH CLICK COUNT

USING GOOGLE RETARGETING

REACH THE 97% THAT DON'T IMMEDIATELY BUY

ANDY SPLICHAL

www.makeeachclickcount.com
www.trueonlinepresence.com
www.makeeachclickcountuniversity.com

Copyrighted Material

Make Each Click Count
Copyright 2021 – By Andy Splichal. All Rights Reserved.
No part of this publication may be reproduced, stored in a retrieval system or transmitted, in any form or by any means – electronic, mechanical, photocopying, recording or otherwise – without prior written permission from the author, except for the inclusion of brief quotations in a review.For information about this title or to order additional copies of this book and/or electronic media, contact the author.

True Online Presence
115 W. California Blvd #311
Pasadena, CA 91105

www.trueonlinepresence.com

info@trueonlinepresence.com

This book, as with all other books in the Make Each Click Count series, is dedicated to my wife, Claudia, and my children, AJ & Charlotte, who continue to fuel me with my inspiration and passion each and every day.

PREFACE

Last year, my wife traveled to Germany to visit her mother, leaving me as a solo dad with my 10-year-old son and 4-year-old daughter.

You know what that means, right?

ROAD TRIP!!

I decided to take the children to Calico Ghost Town. About a 120-mile drive from Pasadena, Calico is a restored silver mining town half-way between Los Angeles and Las Vegas.

In my life BC (before children), I had always noticed the exit for Calico on the many road trips to Las Vegas, and I had always thought of stopping.

Unfortunately, as circumstances would have it, I had always been too excited to stop on the drive towards Las Vegas and too broke and too tired to stop on the drive home.

However, now the time for a Calico ghost town visit was right, and I was not going to miss this opportunity

To celebrate Veterans Day, we awoke bright and early, packed into the car and made the two-and-half hour journey, successfully arriving in Calico.

Some quick history about Calico. Calico was a thriving silver mining town located in the Calico Mountains of the Mojave Desert from 1881 to 1907. In 1951, the town remains were purchased by Walter Knott, the founder of Knott's Berry Farm, when he began to restore Calico to its original condition.

When he was finished in 1966, Walter Knott donated the town to San Bernardino County, and Calico Ghost Town became a Regional Park.

Today, Calico consists of 20 restored buildings (mostly gift shops and restaurants), a small tourist train to ride and a self-guided tour through a restored silver mine.

After spending about 3 hours in Calico, which consisted of riding the train (twice), eating lunch at the Ole' Saloon, visiting absolutely every souvenir store to fully ensure we had selected the perfect Calico remembrance and a trip through the self-guided mining tour, the children and I discovered some important lessons:

For them, they learned that a Ghost Town does not have any actual real ghosts, which we were all a bit disappointed to discover :) and second, that without their mother along, they were limited to picking a single souvenir.

For myself, I was impressed by the self-guided mining tour and, in particular, the story of how two brothers were able to mine out $37,000 worth of silver in about 18 months by using handpicks and dynamite.

Based on inflation and buying power, that would translate into well over $1 million today.

This goes to teach that although technology may change, there will always exist the opportunity for riches.

We are living in a rapidly changing eCommerce landscape as more and more consumer purchases shift from brick-and-mortar stores to online shopping.

In 2020, statistics as reported by CNBC show that consumers spent 9 billion dollars online during Black Friday and $12.3 billion online during Cyber Monday. This is an overall increase of approximately 20% from last year, which coincidentally increased 20% from the year prior to that.

Overall sales for consumers shopping online continue to grow as more and more shoppers become increasingly confident in online purchasing and, in particular, purchases of high-dollar items all from the convenience of shopping from home.

Those silver mining brothers, I am sure, never could had imagined the world we would become 130 years after they handpicked and dynamited their fortune out of 'Dead Man's Gulch.' However, what they did was what many of us strive to do. They used all the resources at their disposal, as well as the opportunity available, to make some serious coin (okay, some serious silver).

Now the question becomes are you effectively using all available marketing channels you can to grab your share of our current proverbial online eCommerce silver rush?

Early in 2020, I released *Make Each Click Count Using Google Shopping.* This book covered the topic of how to create and manage

Google Shopping advertising with the purpose to maximize your sales and profits.

With so many moving parts, including opening a Merchant Center and optimizing bids inside the Google Ads interface while all the time having Google work to switch campaigns to Smart Shopping, it was a much-needed book for eCommerce retailers who were serious about their online marketing.

Now, with my newest book, I work to explain the almost equally misunderstood topic of Google retargeting.

I hope you enjoy, and I hope you use the book to mine out some additional silver in your online marketing.

TABLE OF CONTENTS

PREFACE ---------- v

INTRODUCTION ---------- xiii

Chapter 1 Where To Begin Linking your Google Ads with Google Analytics ---------- 1

Chapter 2 Creating Your Audiences ---------- 6

Chapter 3 Linking Your Remarketing Campaign With Your Data Feed ---------- 16

Chapter 4 Creating A Retargeting Campaign ---------- 24

Chapter 5 Creating High-Converting Retargeting Ads ---------- 33

Chapter 6 Matching Audiences With Google Retargeting Ads ---------- 42

Chapter 7 Opting Out of Google's Sneaky Target Expansion ---------- 47

Chapter 8 Limiting Locations Where Ads Can Appear ---------- 55

Chapter 9 Targeting Where Your Ads Appear ---------- 68

Chapter 10 Frequency - Controlling How Often Your Retargeting Ads Are Shown --- 76

Chapter 11 Adjusting Bids Based On Device ---------------------------- 81

Chapter 12 Measuring the Success of Your Retargeting ------------ 92

Chapter 13 Dotting The I's and Crossing The T's--------------------- 102

INTRODUCTION

M*ake Each Click Count Using Google Retargeting – Reach The 97% That Don't immediately Buy* is your guide to unlocking more sales using Google Retargeting and magnifying profits. The following book reveals step-by-step the latest techniques and strategies typically implemented only by top Google Ad agencies.

On average, only 3% of users that visit a website will make a purchase. A great converting website may double this number to as high as 6%, but even that conversion rate calculates to approximately 19 of 20 people that visit a website and DO NOT purchase.

What if you could continue to effectively market to those proverbial 19 that did not purchase and continue to serve them ads for your website for days, even weeks, after they leave? What if you could even show them ads from your website that included the exact items they were viewing on your website?

You can. It is called retargeting and dynamic retargeting, and this book exists to show you how to do it.

Retargeting vs. Remarketing

Is there a difference between retargeting and remarketing?

The short answer is no. Well, it actually is yes, but no, not really.

Let me clarify.

The terms retargeting and remarketing are often used interchangeably (even by Google), so in that regard, there is no difference. However, technically, there is a difference.

Retargeting is serving ads or 'retargeting' those visitors that have previously visited your website with the purpose of moving them further along your purchase funnel.

Retargeting can be done through the Google Display Network, as is the focus of this book, or through other advertising mediums such as Facebook ads.

Remarketing, on the other hand, is contacting a current or former customer with the purpose of having them reengage with your product or service.

Traditionally done through email, with remarketing you are reaching out to customers who have previously made a purchase from you. Hence, you are 'remarketing' to your customers.

Regardless of definition, these terms have become freely interchangeable. However, for the purpose of this book, we will use the technically correct term of retargeting.

First – How Google Retargeting Ads Work

When a user arrives on a website that has Google Analytics properly installed, a small snippet of code is placed on their browser, referred to as a cookie.

When a user then subsequently leaves and continues to visit other websites that are included in the Google Display Network (GDN), this cookie can be used to display ads to that user by using the data gathered during their initial visit.

The Google Display Network (GDN) where Google retargeting ads are eligible to appear consists of thousands of partnering websites across the internet as well as mobile phone apps and Google-owned sites such as YouTube, Blogger and Gmail.

For each website within the Google Display Network that serves ads, just like with Google Search, there is a real time auction for eligible ads. Google serves eligible ads in designated locations based on how much an individual advertiser is willing to pay if their ad is clicked.

Based on Google's propriety formula, they serve display ads and charge the advertiser if that ad is clicked. Once a user clicks on an ad, they are redirected to the URL of the advertiser's choosing.

If this sounds confusing, don't worry, as we will go into detail on the process within the chapters of this book.

Second – How Google Retargeting Ads Are Set Up

As you probably know, Google Retargeting ads are much different than Google Search ads, the traditional ads that appear on top of Google Search. Also, different is the way that Google Retargeting ads are created.

In order to create a Google Search ad, advertisers create a Google Ads account, create a list of keywords, create an ad, and typically, the ad will be appearing within a couple of hours.

This simplicity to create an ad is one of the reasons that Google Search has become more and more competitive.

Retargeting campaigns are a bit more complicated to create. In order to create a Google Retargeting campaign, advertisers first must install tracking code, use this tracking code to create a group of past website visitors (an audience), and once that audience is large enough, create the ad inside the Google ads interface.

For the advertisers willing to understand and dial in the settings for Google retargeting, they can successfully use Google retargeting to effectively reach and guide website visitors who came to their website but did not purchase further along their purchase funnel.

Won't This Book Become Outdated?

The short answer is YES.

It is hard to believe that it has been almost 6 years since I published my first book – *Make Each Click Count – T.O.P. Guide To Success Using Google Ads* – or almost a full year since I published my second book – *Make Each Click Count Using Google Shopping – Revealing Profits & Strategies*.

In the time since those books were published, the Google interface has changed multiple times.

Some of the terminology has changed. Heck, even the name has changed since the publication of my first book (Google AdWords is now Google Ads).

However, the strategies and underlying fundamentals for both previous books have not changed.

Likewise, with this book, I can promise with absolute certainty that in a year or less (maybe even by the time this book is published), some of Google Ads interface will have changed.

That is just the nature of Google AdWords (excuse me, I meant to say Google Ads).

However, what won't change are the advanced strategies on how to strategically create your audiences and write effective retargeting ads.

What Does This Book Contain?

- This book contains everything you need to know to successfully create and optimize effective Google Retargeting campaigns.
- **Where To Begin** – Creating your retargeting audience using Google Analytics and linking Google Analytics with your Google Ads account.
- **Create Your First Google Retargeting Campaign** – Creating a retargeting campaign can be confusing. If you don't select the proper settings, you could just be creating a non-effective display campaign instead of targeting past website users.
- **Creating Effective Retargeting Ads** – The purpose of retargeting is to draw past website visitors back to your website. To do this, you will need to know the best-practices creating effective retargeting ads.
- **Dialing In The Settings** – This is what typically sets apart professionals from novices when it comes to Google retargeting. Discover what settings are important and how to manage those settings properly for optimal results.

How Should You Read This Book?

How to read this book is going to depend on you and what you want to take from the book. Reading the book in order, cover-to-cover, while taking notes and marking pages will lead to some great insights. It will also most likely bring a perspective you have never thought about – even for the most experienced advertiser. I am confident that this book will provide you with a complete understanding of advanced techniques and strategies involved with Google retargeting.

Even for the advertiser just starting with Google retargeting, this book will lead them through a journey from inception to completion, providing the ultimate goal of creating and maintaining successful Google retargeting campaigns.

If you are pressed for time, start reading the chapter that details where you currently need help in your account. However, make sure you return to read the full book as this book was written as a working book, not a workbook!

Why Did I Write This Book?

My name is Andy Splichal, and I have been managing Google Ads campaigns for almost twenty years! Since 2001, I've managed hundreds of thousands of dollars for my clients.

Since 2014, I have managed Google Ads for private clients through True Online Presence, where I continue to be the Founder & Managing Partner.

True Online Presence is a partnered Google Ads agency that continually strives to provide profits through best-practices and cutting-edge proprietary strategies for our private clients using Search, Shopping and Display ads.

Since publishing my first book in 2015 – *Make Each Click Count – T.O.P. Guide To Success Using Google Shopping – the* opportunity for profitability continues to shift quickly, leaving companies that would like to manage their own Google Ads struggling to keep up.

This struggle is why I decided to write *Make Each Click Count Using Google Shopping* and now this book, *Make Each Click Count Using Google Retargeting*. The Make Each Click Count book series was created to share with you how we at True Online Presence create and optimize various pieces of Google advertising for our private clients.

For those willing to put in the work to not only read this book, but to understand and apply the techniques taught, I invite you to continue reading.

By finishing this book and implementing what you discover, you will be ready to enjoy the same level of success using Google advertising typically reserved for private Google partner agencies with years of experience!

I hope you enjoy the book.

Andy Splichal

Chapter 1

Where To Begin Linking Your Google Ads With Google Analytics

Once you have made the decision to start doing any type of advertising using Google, the first step entails opening a Google Ads account.

Creating a Google Ads account is quite simple.

In order to create a new Google Ads account, navigate to ads.google.com. Once there, Google will guide you through opening an account through a series of questions regarding your goals and information about the website you plan to advertise and guide you through how to create your first search ads.

In addition, most business owners, before they start spending money on advertising, want the ability to see how well their ads perform.

Common metrics for measuring a campaign's profitability include ROAS (return on ad spend) and ROI (return on investment). These metrics can be calculated by implementing Google Ads tracking to your website.

However, used alone, Google Ads tracking won't give you the full picture of how Google paid traffic interacted with your website, and it won't provide any data on how other non-paid visitors interact with your website. In order to gather this data, you need to create and setup an additional Google Analytics account.

In order to create a new Google Analytics account, navigate to analytics.google.com. Again, Google will guide you through the steps to create your new Google Analytics account, including where to place tracking code on your website.

After you create and set up your Google Analytics, you will want to ensure that your Google Ads account and Google Analytics account communicate with each other. For this, you will want to make sure you link the two accounts.

Linking Google Ads and Google Analytics accounts allows advertisers to view the full picture of their website traffic through the following ways:

Viewing Google Ad performance within Google Analytics.

The ability to import transactions and goals from Google Analytics to Google Ads.

The ability to import certain metrics not available in Google Ads such as bounce rate and pages/session from Google Analytics to Google Ads.

And, for the purpose of retargeting, it will allow us to use audiences created in Google Analytics within our Google Ads account when creating our retargeting campaigns

In next chapter, we will look at the specific steps for creating audiences. For now, we look at the process of how to link your two accounts.

Linking Google Ads With Google Analytics

Before you can link accounts, you need to ensure you have certain permission levels for each account. For Google Ads, you will need Edit permission. For Google Analytics, you will need administrative access. In addition, the Google Ads account will need to be currently active in order to eligible to link.

1. Sign into Google Analytics.
2. Click Admin (lower left corner) and navigate to the property you want to link.
3. In the Property column, click Google Ads Linking.
4. Click '+ New link group.'
5. Select the Google Ads accounts you want to link, then click Continue.
6. Enter a link group title.
7. Turn All Web Site Data ON for each view in the property in which you want Google Ads data.
8. Click on 'Share my Analytics data with linked Google accounts.'

Note, if you want to manually tag your Google Ads links, click 'Advanced Settings' and select 'leave auto-tagging settings as they are.'

9. Click Link accounts.

WHERE TO BEGIN LINKING YOUR GOOGLE ADS WITH GOOGLE ANALYTICS

Once you click link accounts, your accounts should be linked. When linking, if you used auto-tagging, then your Google Analytics account will start automatically associating data received with your Google Ads tracking with user clicks and traffic inside Google Analytics.

Google Ads will also be eligible to begin using the audiences that we are going to create within our Google Analytics account

Final Word

A basic but necessary step linking Google Analytics with Google Ads allows for the full collection and sharing of data. It will also be requirefor us to properly use retargeting with audiences created in Google Analytics.

It is advised to link your accounts immediately, but if you have been running Google Ads accounts for some time and have not yet linked, you still can have the ability to make that link.

Unfortunately, you won't have the past data from Google Ads appear inside Google Analytics, but the data from Google ads will start appearing inside Google Analytics once you link the accounts.

And for our purpose of retargeting, you will have the ability to begin retargeting once we complete the next few steps in the coming chapters.

Chapter 2

Creating Your Audiences

hen you think about creating ads within Google, typically you would assume the first step would take place within the Google Ads interface.

After all, isn't Google Analytics just for tracking?

And while it is true that Google Analytics is a vital tool for tracking, it has evolved over the last few years into much more for advertisers in terms of capturing information and recycling that data for practical use.

Once created, retargeting ads will be eligible to serve across the Google Display Network (the GDN). The GDN is a collection of websites that includes Google owned websites such as YouTube, Gmail, Google Finance, Blogger as well as thousands of other non-Google sites, mobile sites and apps.

What differentiates true retargeting (marketing to specific users who have visited your website) from Google display advertising is that ads are only shown to those users who have previously interacted with their website.

In order to apply these types of restrictive rules on ads, advertisers first must create what Google refers to as an audience. An audience defines how users have previously interacted with a website and in what timeframe.

Creating your audience will include naming, identifying the advertising account which you want to use and creating the criteria for the audience, which will all be done within Google Analytics.

Note, there is a maximum of 50 audiences that you can publish and define within each Google Analytics account, which typically will be plenty for most advertisers.

Now that we know what an audience is and how we are going to use it, the next step we will look at is how to properly configure.

Modifying Property Settings

Before we create our first audience, we need to modify the data collection settings within Google Analytics.

Here are the steps:

1. Sign-in to your Analytics account.
2. Click Admin (lower left corner) and navigate to the property column for which you want to enable these features.
3. In the Property column, click Tracking Info, then click Data Collection.
4. Under Data Collection for Advertising Features:

5. To enable Remarketing, set Remarketing and Advertising Reporting Features to ON.

- To enable only the Advertising Reporting Features, set only Advertising Reporting Features to ON.

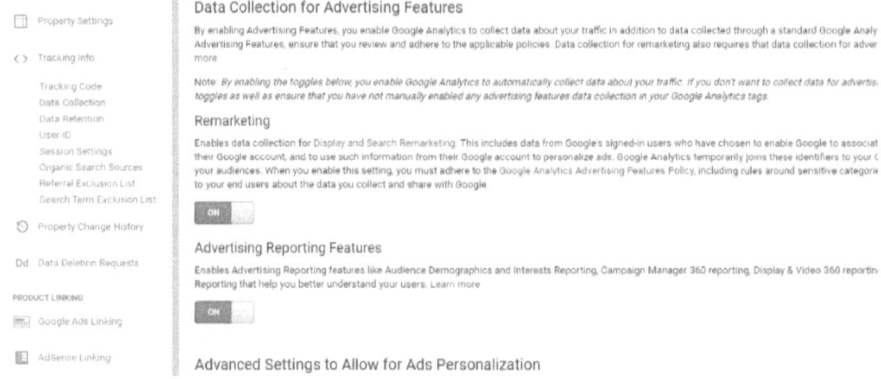

Once you have the data collections settings enabled, you are ready to move onto creating your first audience.

Creating Your Audiences

Once you have enabled the data collection through your Analytics account, you will be able to start creating your audiences.

By adding your Google Analytics pixel to your website and enabling the option to collect data, you are allowing Google to place a cookie (a small bit of snippet) on the browser of users that visit your website.

Again, audiences is the grouping that Google uses to define a specific group of users. We as advertisers have the ability to group our specific website visitors inside our audiences by how they interact with our website aka their session-based behavior.

With Google collecting the data, advertisers have the ability to define their audiences based in both broad terms (those that visited your website in the past xx days) to more granular terms (those that visited a specific website page) and almost any actions visitors have taken in between.

First, we will look at how to create an audience and then we will look at the possibilities of defining audiences.

Steps to create an audience:

1. Sign into your Google Analytics account.
2. Click 'Admin' the gear icon in the lower left corner.
3. Within the Property column, click on Audience Definitions > Audiences.
4. Click on the +New Audience button.

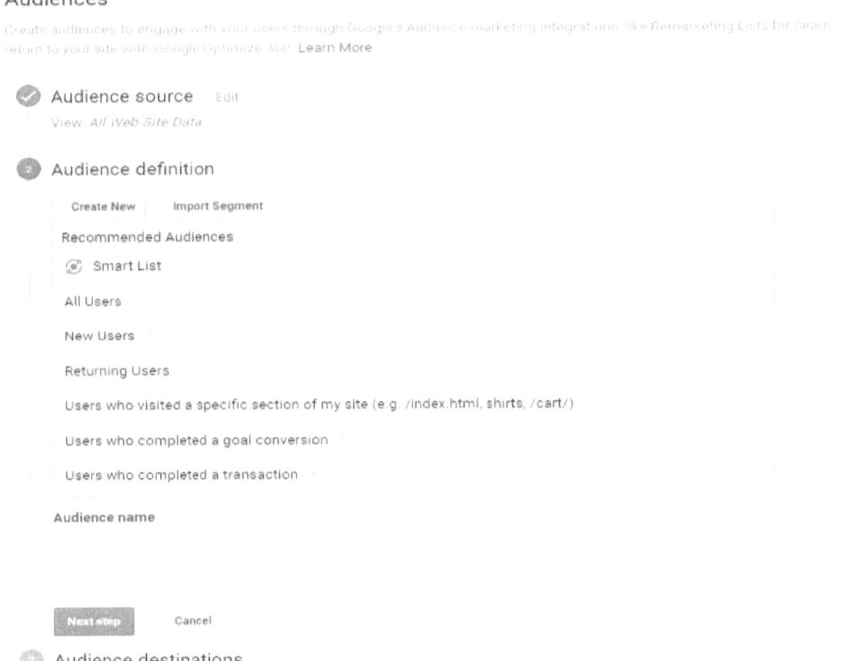

Creating an audience has three steps: Audience source, Audience definition and Audience destination.

Audience Source – The audience source is the first-party data source where advertisers are going to pull the data that they will put into an audience. Before you can use, most audience sources require that you link your Google ads account with the audience source account.

Different audience sources include Google Ads tag, Google Analytics, YouTube, Google Play, App Analytics and Customer data.

For most eCommerce retailers, your most effective audience source will be Google Analytics and pulling data based on the Google Analytics tracking tag.

Audience Definitions - Once you have defined where to pull your data, the next step is to define how to create your audiences. This is where we as advertisers really have the ability to earn our stripes as advanced marketers!

Through Google Analytics, you will have the ability to create audiences in a multitude of ways all based on how someone interacted with your website using Google's Audience Builder.

From the length of visit to how many purchases, pages visited, what pages they visited, to even the traffic source that directed them to your website, marketers have the ability to slice and dice their data in order to later serve targeted ads based on different interactions.

Just note, before you go and get too granular with creating your audiences, a remarketing audience currently must include a minimum of 100 unique cookies in order for Google to serve ads to that audience within the Google Display Network.

If you wish to use a remarketing list to enhance your search ads, Google requires a minimum of 1,000 unique cookies. These minimum limits are the same whether using Google Ads or Google Analytics tracking pixels.

Therefore, however you define your audience, there must be sufficient members of the audience gathered before you will be able to use an audience within a remarketing campaign.

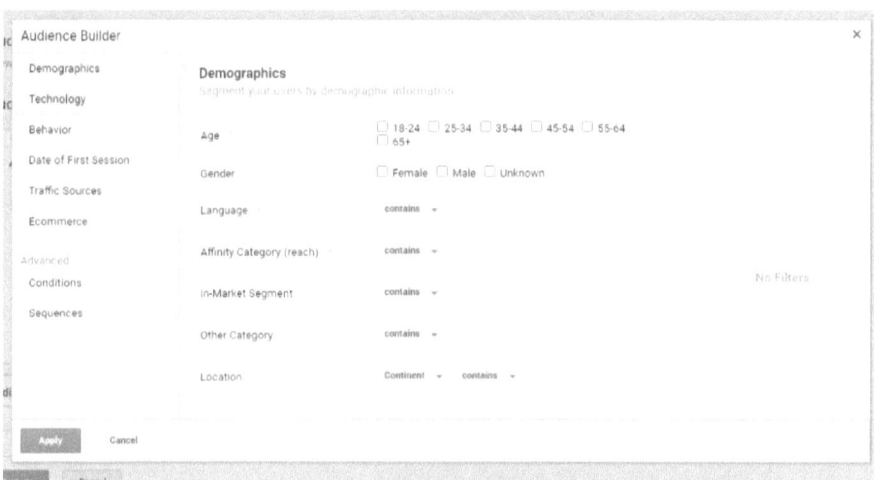

Once you have defined your audience, named your audience (a name that will help you easily keep remember how you defined the audience), the last step is to decide where to share your audience.

Audience Destinations

When you select your audience destination, you are choosing the destination where you would like your audience to be able to be used. Although it sounds simple, make sure you set it up correctly because you cannot change the destination for Google Ads destinations after you publish your audience.

To add the destination, click on the +Add destinations button and choose where you would like your audience to be shared, aka published.

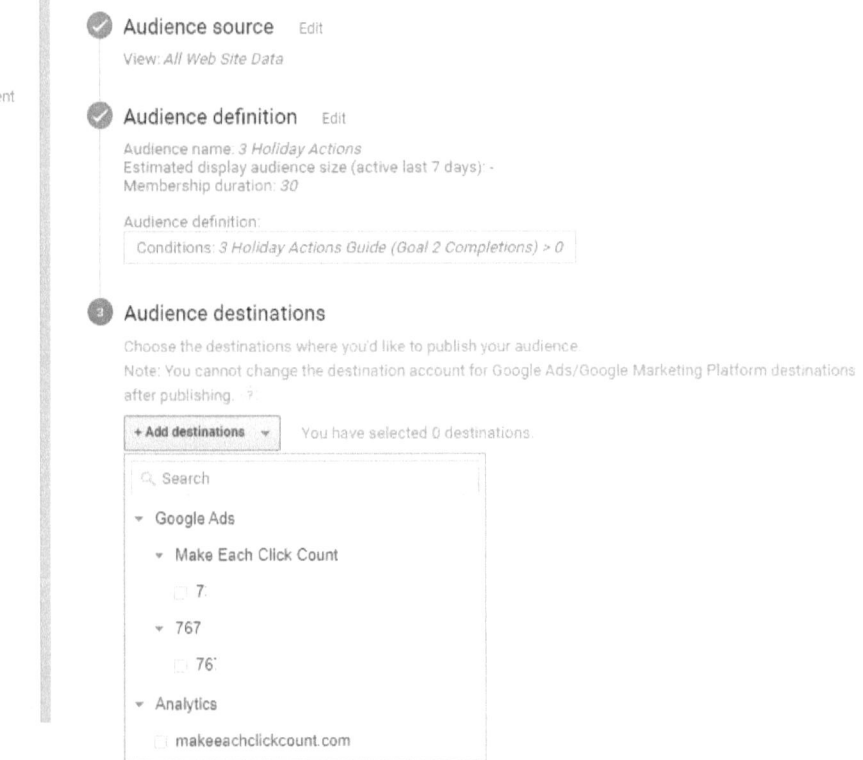

Note, your Google Analytics accounts will automatically be included; however, in order for your Google Ads account to be listed as a destination you will first need to have linked your Google Analytics with your Google Ads account.

If you do not see your Google Ads account listed, the most likely cause is that your Analytics and Google Ads accounts are not linked. In order to properly link, review the previous chapter, "Where To Begin - Linking your Google Ads with Google Analytics."

The Audience Manager

Once you have created multiple audiences within Google Analytics, Google allows you to quickly set up, manage and monitor your audiences and audience sources within the Google Ads interface using the Audience Manager.

We will go into more details regarding ways to specifically use Google's audience manager later in the book. However, you should be aware that it is a useful tool to discover more data regarding existing audiences such as data on users who make up your audiences including demographics, interests, location and devices.

Google's audience manager is helpful in easily managing audiences. In addition, it allows for easy creation of new audiences and for creating audiences from sources other than your Google Analytics tags such as YouTube, Google Play and Customer data.

As of now, the Google audience manager doesn't have all of the functionality in segmenting actions when defining an audience. This limitation is why I recommend you begin creating your audiences in Google Analytics with the goal of using past website behavior to create your audiences.

However, advertisers should be aware of the audience manager and how to access it in order to easily manage audiences.

Accessing Your Google Audience Manager -

1. Login to Google Ads Account.
2. Click on Tools & Settings (top menu).
3. Click on Audience Manager under Shared Library.

The Audience manager is subdivided into 3 sections: Audience sources, Audience lists, and Audience insights. We will discuss more regarding how to use these later within the book.

Final Word

Creating an audience is a powerful way to group your website visitors based on how interested they may be in purchasing your products.

This level of interest can be referred to as the purchase funnel.

If you think of it like a pyramid, on the bottom are people that briefly looked at your website (perhaps under 10 seconds) and then left.

Next are visitors that may have looked at an item page for xxx amount of time (over a minute perhaps).

Higher than that are visitors you looked at multiple pages on your website while still spending XXX amount of time (over a minute perhaps).

One step higher are visitors that added an item to the cart, then those visitors that continued to the shipping/billing page, and finally, those visitors that purchased an item.

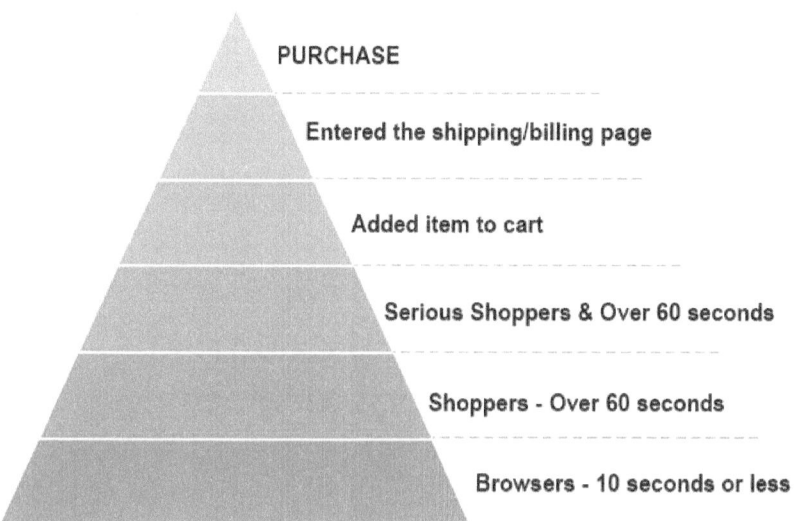

Our goal when creating an audience should be to create different audiences based on the different levels of the purchase funnel.

The reason to segment the purchase funnel into different audiences is that we can later decide which audiences we will want to serve retargeting ads, and we will be able to bid differently based on where a user lands within the funnel.

As you probably figured out, the closer a past visitor came to the top of the funnel, the more likely they will be to purchase from your retargeting ads.

And this is the importance of correctly creating your audiences!

Chapter 3

Linking Your Remarketing Campaign With Your Data Feed

Have you ever been on a webpage and noticed an advertisement for the exact product that you had previously viewed while on a different website?

This is dynamic retargeting.

Dynamic retargeting is the ability to serve unique ads to users based on each user's past engagement.

The difference between retargeting and dynamic retargeting?

Retargeting allows advertisers to serve ads to users who have visited their website. These users can be segmented into audiences based on some action they performed while on your website. Actions may include visiting certain page such as the cart, length of time, how many pages visited, etc.

However, those ads are static, meaning that all ads have the same images and once clicked, the ads direct users to the same static URL.

As a difference, dynamic retargeting ads allow advertisers to pair their Google Merchant Center feed to their ads. This allows ads to include the images linked to the URLs of actual products that a user viewed while on your site.

Best of all, once you connect your data feed from Google Merchant Center with your Google Retargeting Campaign, this ability to use dynamic retargeting works seamlessly and is highly effective.

Google uses their algorithm to predict which dynamic layout is best to perform for each user, including taking into consideration the placement and platform for where your ads will appear.

Linking Your Data Feed

First thing's first. Before you can connect your data feed to your Google campaign, you first must have an active data feed inside your Google Merchant Center account.

If you don't have a Google Merchant Center Account, then you cannot create a dynamic retargeting campaign. You also cannot create a Google Shopping campaign.

Within my book, *Make Each Click Count Using Google Shopping*, I dedicate an entire section, including 3 chapters, to the process of creating and optimizing your Google Merchant Center and subsequent data feed.

For our purpose, we will assume that you have your Google Merchant Center feed in place and are now looking to connect your data feed with a retargeting campaign.

In link a data feed to a campaign, there are two steps that you will need to take:

Step 1 – Link Google Merchant Center Account with Google Ads Account.

Step 2 – Link the data feed to our Google Retargeting Campaign.

Step 1 - Link Google Merchant Center Account with Google Ads Account.

1. Open Google Merchant Center.
2. Click on the Wrench icon in the upper right navigation bar of Merchant Center.
3. Select Linked Accounts.
4. Click Link Account and enter your Google Ads ID and press 'Send Link Request'.

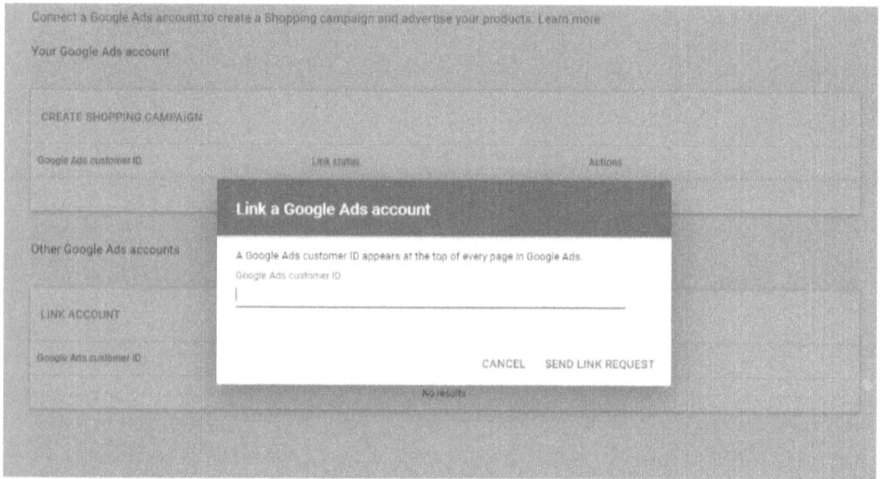

5. Next, we need to open our Google Ads Account.
6. Click on the Wrench icon in the upper right navigation bar of Google Ads account.

7. Click on Linked Accounts located under 'Settings.'
8. Scroll down under Google Merchant Center and click on the Details link.
9. There you will see your pending invitation to connect to your Google Merchant Center.

10. Click on view details and approve the invitation.

Congratulations, you have now connected your Merchant Center and Google Ads account and are ready to connect your data feed.

Step 2 - Link Data Feed to Google Retargeting Campaign.

Here are the steps to add a data feed to an existing retargeting campaign:

1. Sign into your Google Ads Account and click on the Campaign Settings.
2. Click on Additional Settings.

3. Click on the Drop-Down Menu under Dynamic Ads. Note, by default it is set to 'No Data Feed.'
4. Change the selection to select your Google Merchant Center Data Feed.
5. Select the checkbox for 'use dynamic ads feed for personalized ads.'
6. Select the data feed that you wish to link from the drop-down menu.
7. Select whether or not to use Product filters, which will determine which products are eligible to be included in your dynamic ads.
8. Click Save.

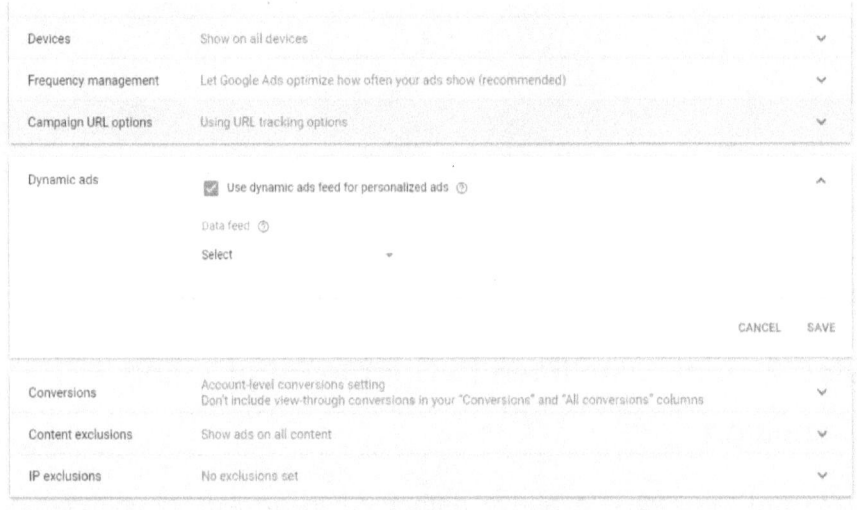

Once you save, you should see that next to Dynamic Ads appears "With Data Feed.'

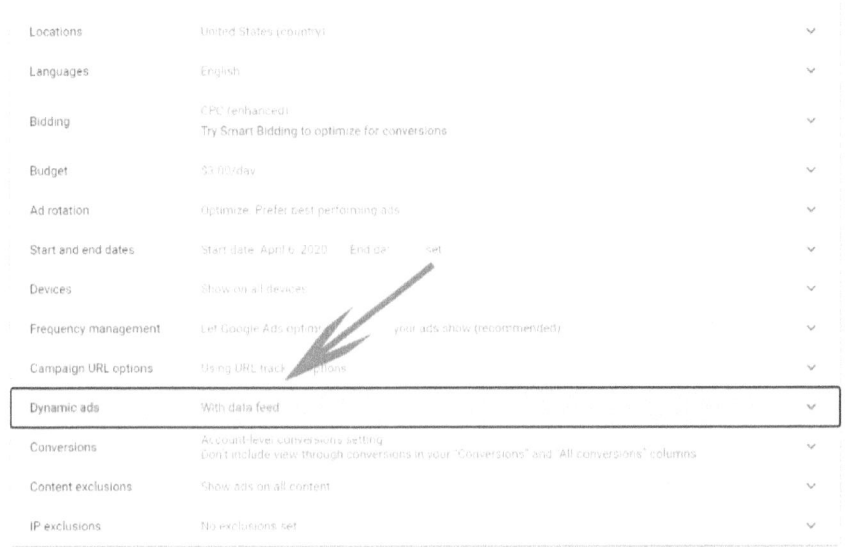

Here are the steps to add a data feed to a new retargeting campaign:

1. Sign into your Google Ads account.
2. Click **Campaigns** from the page menu.
3. Click the plus button ⊕ to create a new campaign.
4. Choose your campaign goal of Sales and click Continue.
5. Select **Display** as the campaign type.
6. Select 'standard display campaign' and your business website.
7. Name your campaign and specify locations, languages, bidding, and budget.
8. Under Additional Settings, Dynamic Ads, you can link your Google Feed by clicking on the drop-down ad. **Note, by default it is set to 'No Data Feed.'**
9. Your selections in the "Targeting" section is where dynamic remarketing comes in. If you want to target specific audiences only, set targeting to "Manual" to choose audience groups in

LINKING YOUR REMARKETING CAMPAIGN WITH YOUR DATA FEED

the audiences menu. This is where you can determine only to include audiences that you have created out of visitors in how they have interacted with your website. Once you've manually selected a list from the list options, click **Done**. Also, remember, unless you opt out of "Targeting expansion," Google will automatically serve your ads to like users similar to the defined audience you selected (I recommend turning off for retargeting ads).

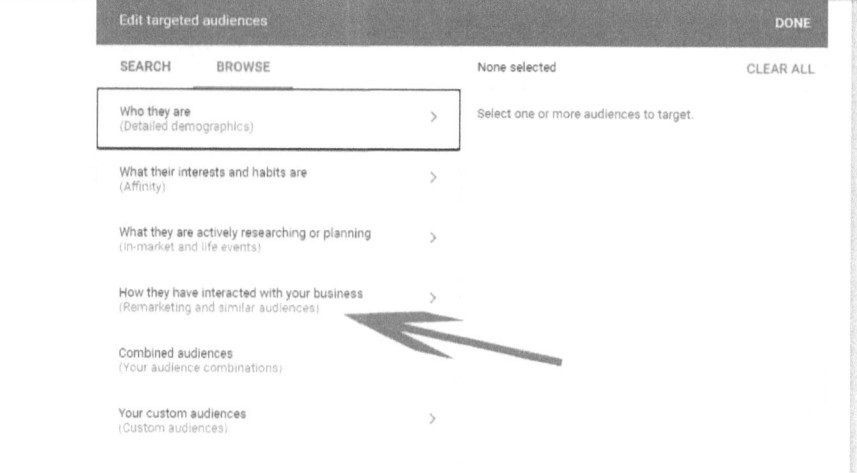

10. Create and save your Display ads.
11. Click Create campaign.

Note, the next chapter will detail the steps creating a new retargeting campaign from scratch.

Final Word

Dynamic retargeting ads are a powerful way to stay connected to users that visit your website but did not purchase. The power of these type of ads are created by their high relevancy to the user.

Because you can display the actual product that a customer was already viewing on your website, you know they have interest.

If they have interest, why didn't they buy, you might ask?

Who really knows?

Maybe they were price shopping. Maybe they got busy. Maybe they just weren't ready.

Regardless of the reason, they do have interest, as you can determine by their past actions on your website, and by being able to stay in front of those customers, you can make sure that they remember who you are and that you carry the product that they want.

You will also ensure that you are there when the customer is ready to buy.

Chapter 4

Creating A Retargeting Campaign

Assuming that you have now linked your Google Ads account with your Google Analytics account and created audiences within your Google Analytics account, you are now ready to create a Google Retargeting campaign.

Remember, before you get too excited, you need to have a minimum of 100 unique cookies before an audience will be eligible to receive your retargeting ads. Therefore, if you have recently created an audience, you may have to wait until there are at least 100 users before ads will begin serving.

However, there is nothing from preventing you from creating the campaign while you wait for your audiences to populate.

Steps to create a Retargeting campaign:

1. Sign in to your Google Ads account.
2. Click blue plus button  and select New Campaign.
3. Select your campaign's goal – 'Sales' is the standard selection

4. Select your campaign type – 'Display' is the option for retargeting ads.
5. Select your campaign subtype – 'Standard display campaign' – Note, Google will recommend their Smart display campaign – Don't do it! You won't be allowed the function of customizing settings in order to optimize your campaign's profitability described later in this book. Also note, if you select Smart display campaign, you cannot change later. You will need to recreate a new Standard display campaign.

6. Enter your business website and click CONTINUE.
7. Name your campaign.
8. Select the location(s) where you want your ads to be eligible to appear.
9. Select the language that your customers speak.

CREATING A RETARGETING CAMPAIGN

10. Set your bidding. Note, again, Google will recommend their automated bidding strategies. When running retargeting campaigns, I use defined audiences based on the purchase funnel as discussed in the last chapter. Therefore, select a direct bid strategy (even though Google will try to discourage this option).

11. Click on 'set bid strategy directly.'

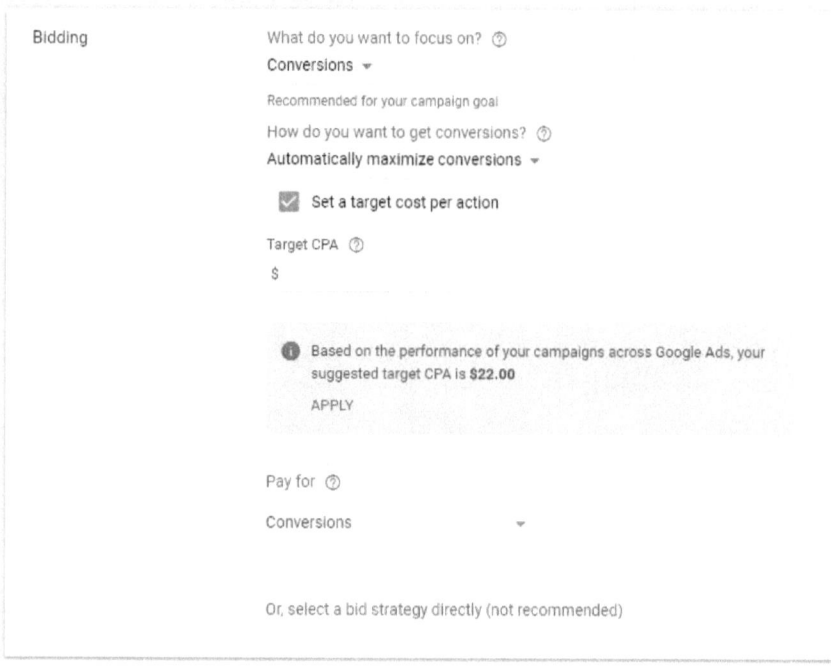

12. I also recommend setting your own bids using Manual CPC rather than relying on Google's automated bid strategies. However, the campaign's bidding strategy can be changed after inception, so advertisers are able to test what provides the best results over time.

MAKE EACH CLICK COUNT USING GOOGLE RETARGETING

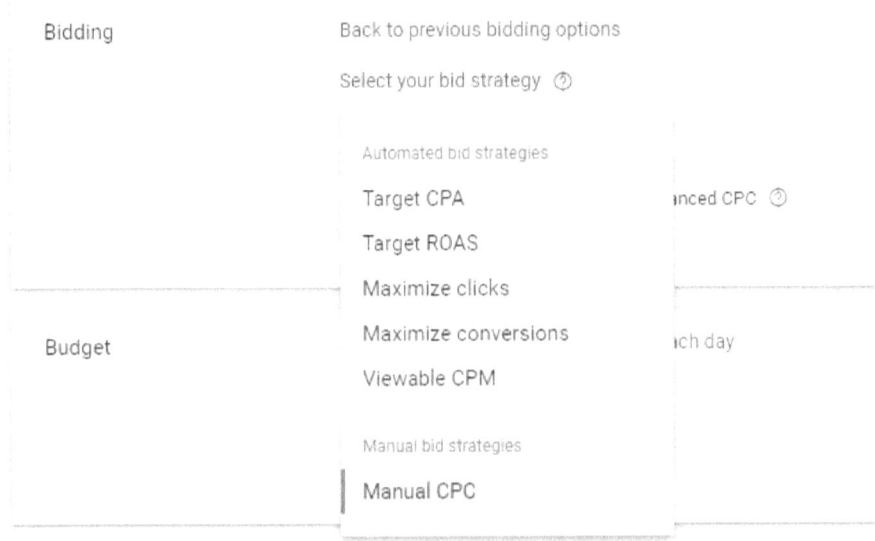

13. Set your budget.
14. Name your ad group.
15. Select your audience.

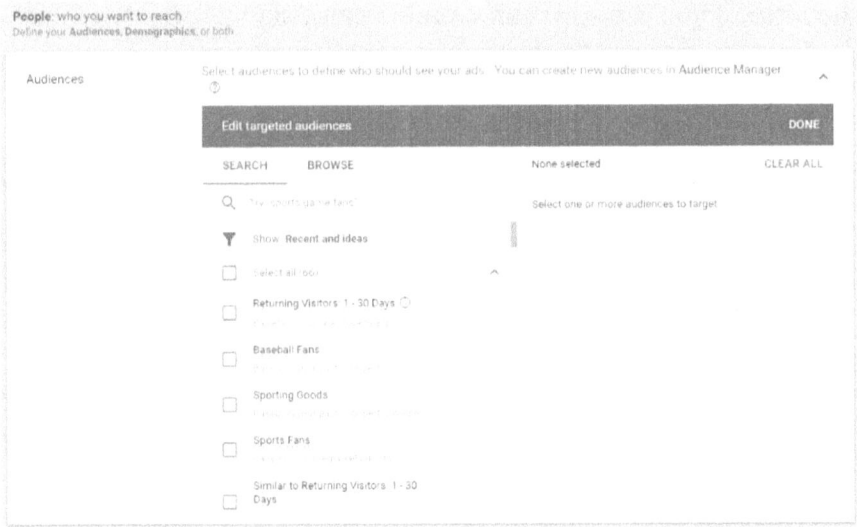

Selecting A Campaign's Audience

Matching your desired audience is the most essential step in correctly running your retargeting campaign. It is the audience that will determine for which group of website visitors your retargeting ads are going to be eligible to appear. It is also the use of an audience that differentiates a retargeting campaign from a normal display campaign.

Since selecting an audience is so essential, I have broken down the process of selecting an audience into its own section even though it is a part of the initial campaign creation.

When you first arrive at the Edit target audience box, the current default is to show search. Search displays Google-recommended audiences matching their library with your website as well as audiences that may have been previously used.

Of course, if you like, you can create a campaign using any of these audiences that Google automatically suggests, but that will not be retargeting; instead, it will be display advertising.

Remember, in order to create dynamic retargeting, our end game is to serve ads that have specific products to a user that they viewed while on our website.

Therefore, instead of using Search, we want to select Browse and navigate to 'How they have interacted with your business,' then 'Website visitors.'

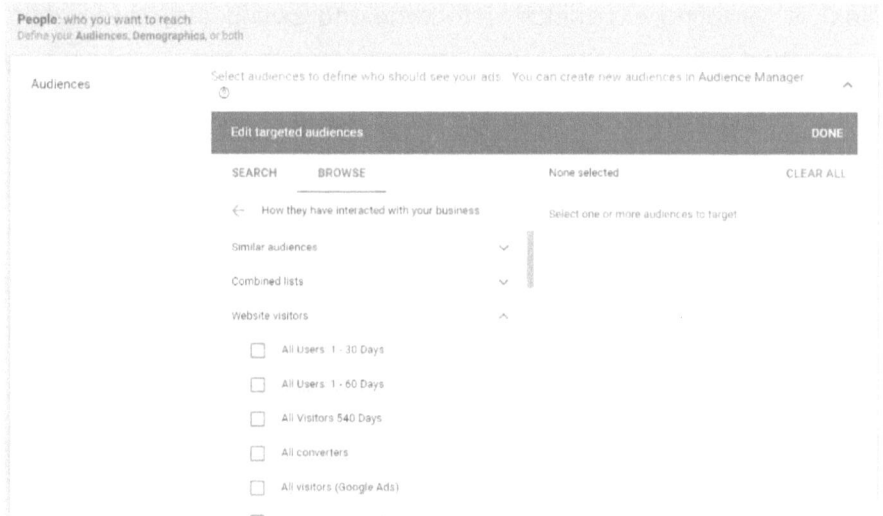

If you have correctly linked your Google Ads and Google Analytics accounts and properly created audiences as detailed in the past two chapters, you should see your custom audiences then appear.

Select the audience you wish to target in the ad group you are creating and click done.

Next, you have the option to edit your targeted demographics. This is ideal for targeting specific ages, genders, incomes, etc. However, since we are serving ads to previous website visitors, this option is not relevant to retargeting ads.

Working with demographics is important when working with true display ads where the audience you are using are not aware of your business. In that scenario, segmenting for demographics becomes extremely beneficial in pinpointing your ideal customer by age, gender, parental status or household income.

However, for retargeting ads, it is not needed, so you can skip this section.

Next is targeting expansion. I recommend opting out of targeting expansion as we are setting up the campaign. Opting out of target expansion will allow the soon-to-be created campaign to only serve ads to past visitors as we identified with our selected audience. I go into full detail in Chapter 7 regarding target expansion, but for now, you can be comfortable turning the slider to off.

Next, create your ad group bid. Since we have changed the bid strategy to manual CPC, we must now determine the bid for your ad group. The bid is easily changed once the campaign is created, but for now, a bid must be entered.

Google provides an estimate of campaigns with similar targeting below the bid box as well as weekly estimates to the right of the bid box. However, in the past, I have not found these to be accurate and generally will set the ad group bid significantly lower than what Google recommends.

The next step is to attach your data feed. This will allow Google to pull product data from your product feed and use that data to create your dynamic ads.

To attach your product feed, simply click on the box 'Use dynamic ads feed for personalized ads' and select the appropriate data feedNote, if the Merchant Center Account does not appear under the data feed drop down, this typically means you did not correctly link your Google Merchant Center Account with your Google Ads Account.

Finally, we are ready to create our responsive display ad. This ad will be what your audience is shown and ultimately what determines if past users return to your website.

This process should not be taken lightly as it will be vital to the success of your retargeting campaign.

It is so vital that I have dedicated the entire next chapter to constructing your ads. Typically, I don't recommend skipping around the book, but here I make an exception. Read this chapter NOW to ensure you create a solid retargeting ad.

Once you have created your ad, click on the 'Create Campaign' button, and you are done.

Congratulations, your retargeting campaign has been created! Once your ad is approved, you will begin to serve your approved ads to the audience that you have selected.

Final Word

As you go through each of the steps in this chapter, you may be confused as there are many steps. In fact, by the time you read these words, Google may have very well changed the order of the settings or how some of the settings appear.

The important takeaway from this chapter is to keep your end game in mind - to serve ads that have specific products that a user viewed while on our website to those previous website visitors.

If you keep that end goal in mind, the steps will make sense regardless of whether Google's interface changes.

You must name your campaign/ad group, set the maximum you are willing to pay per ad if clicked, how much to spend per day, select who you would like to be eligible to be served your ads and create your ads.

Once created, you will be able to change any of the above configurations, so don't worry too much about making a mistake when initially creating.

Go ahead and create your new retargeting campaigns, and later, we will continue to look at how to tweak our settings in order to optimize it for success.

Chapter 5

Creating High-Converting Retargeting Ads

Once you have created your retargeting campaign and properly configured your initial settings, the next and maybe most important step is to create your retargeting ad.

The retargeting ad is perhaps the most important piece of the retargeting puzzle. If you do not have an engaging retargeting ad, then it won't matter what audience you target or how you configure your settings.

During the initial campaign setup, you have the ability to create your retargeting ad(s). Alternatively, you can either add new ads or update existing ads once the campaign and the ad group have already been created.

For retargeting or any other type of Google display ads, the only type of ad that Google currently supports is the responsive display ad.

This is a bit of a relief. Before the responsive display ad, Google remarketing advertisers would need to format between 12-15 various sized ads with matching images for each.

Today, the responsive display ads automatically will adjust an ad's size, appearance and format to match the available ad space.

To create a responsive display ad, advertisers will enter various assets including logos, headlines, images, videos (optional) and descriptions and let Google handle the optimizing all the provided assets for the best performance.

Here are the steps as provided by Google to create a responsive display ad:

1. Sign in to your Google Ads account.
2. From the navigation panel on the left, select **Display campaigns**.
3. Then click **Ads & extensions** from the page menu on the left.
4. Click blue plus button ⊕.
5. Select **Responsive display ad**.
6. Select the ad group for which you wish to create your ad. If you want your responsive display ads to support dynamic remarketing, make sure your ad group, or its campaign, is attached to a feed.
7. Add and save your images. To give you access to all ad formats, images are required. Having multiple assets is recommended because it makes it easier for Google to optimize your ads. You can upload up to 15 marketing images and 5 logos. You can crop a single image to the landscape and square formats or use separate images for each aspect ratio.

8. Upload your images, scan them from your website, or select from our free library of professional stock images. You can also select from recently used images.
    a. **Landscape**. If you choose the upload option, keep in mind that your landscape image should have a ratio of 1.91:1 and be greater than 600 x 314. The file size limit is 5120KB.
    b. **Square**. If you choose the upload option, keep in mind that your square (1:1) image should be greater than 300 x 300. The file size limit is 5120KB.
    c. **Logo (optional)**. If you choose the upload option, keep in mind that your logo should be square (1:1) and should be 128 x 128 or greater. The recommended size for the square logo is 1200 x 1200. For best rendering, it is also recommended to add a landscape (4:1) logo, which should be 512 x 128 or greater. The recommended size for the landscape logo is 1200 x 300. For all your logos, a transparent background is best, but only if the logo is centered. The file size limit is 5120KB.
    d. **Avoid text**. Text may cover no more than 20% of the image. **Note:** To fit in some ad spaces, your image may be cropped horizontally—up to 5% on each side.
9. Click on ⊕ **Videos** below "Images and Logos".
10. Ensure the video you'd like to show has been uploaded to YouTube. Then add YouTube links by searching for a video

11. or paste the URL from YouTube. If you choose the upload option, keep in mind the preferred length of the video (recommended aspect ratios: 16:9, 1:1, 4:3, 9:16) should be 30 seconds or less. Only YouTube video links are permitted for the ad.
12. Complete your ad information. You can create multiple headlines and descriptions to be rendered in your responsive display ads. You can upload multiple versions of the following:

    a. Write a **short headline** (at least 1, or up to 5 headlines, of 30 characters or fewer). The short headline is the first line of your ad and appears in tight ad spaces where the long headline doesn't fit. Short headlines may appear with or without your description inside your ads.

    b. Write a **long headline** (90 characters or fewer). The long headline is the first line of your ad and appears instead of your short headline in larger sized ads. Long headlines may appear with or without your description. **Note:** When rendered in an ad, the long headline's length will depend on the site it appears on. If shortened, the long headline will end with ellipses.

    c. Write a **description** (at least 1 is required and up to 5 descriptions are allowed). The description adds to the headline and invites people to take action. It can be up to 90 characters and may appear after the (short or long) headline. Note: The length of the rendered description will depend on the site it appears on. If shortened, the description will end with ellipses.

d. **Business name.** This is the name of your business or brand.

e. **Final URL.** This is where people will go when they click on your ad.

f. Optional: Go to **advanced URL options** to add tracking or custom parameters to your URL.

g. Optional: Click **MORE OPTIONS** and select **Call to action text**. From the drop-down menu (on the left) select a language, and from the drop-down menu (on the right) select a specific call to action text.

h. Optional for dynamic responsive ads: **promotion text** (for example, "Free two-day shipping") and **price prefix**.

13. Preview the most popular sizes and ad formats of your potential ads. Since responsive display ads are built to reach across almost any ad space on the Display Network, they can show in thousands of layouts.

14. Click **Save**.

Following the steps is the easy part. Now that you know what to do, selecting images and creating effective headlines and descriptions is what is going to make your retargeting ads perform.

Remember, when you are using display ads, you are no longer advertising to those actively searching for your products.

When you use retargeting, you will be advertising to those who have previously visited your website; therefore, they are at least are familiar with your company. However, they are still not actively searching for your products at the time they see your ads.

Therefore, your ads must be written a bit differently from normal Google Search Ads. In short, they must be disruptive. Images need to be eye catching; headlines need to be exciting and full of benefits. They need to be created with the purpose of pulling attention from whatever the user was previously doing into clicking on your ad.

Videos are a relatively new concept in the retargeting ads but have been extremely beneficial in increasing click through rates with my private clients. The videos automatically play within the ads and are disruptive by nature with their movement. In order to add a video, the video must first be uploaded into YouTube as you will need to add the YouTube link in order to link a video to a responsive display ad.

Rules For Creating Responsive Display Ads

When creating a dynamic response ad, there are required elements and best-practices.

With the dynamic responsive ad type, Google allows advertisers to upload more images, headlines and descriptions than are required. Uploading more than is required is a real benefit of this ad type. By uploading as many images, videos (optional), headlines and descriptions as possible, you will allow Google to mix and match, helping Google's algorithm determine the optimal results.

Here is a list of required elements as well as the maximum number of elements currently supported:

- FINAL URL (Just 1). This is where the ad will direct a user when they click on the ad. Note, if dynamic retargeting is set up, then the products displayed within the ad when clicked will lead directly to the product's URL.
- IMAGES & LOGOS – Minimum of 1 Square and 1 landscape. Maximum of 15 images and 5 logos. Google has made the process of uploading images and logos easy to navigate. Google will scan your website and social media feeds for relevant images. You can upload your own images or if all else fails you can use stock images.
- VIDEOS – Optional, but up to 5 videos can be included within each ad.
- HEADLINES – Up to 5. Headlines have a maximum of 30 characters.
- LONG HEADLINE – This appears as the first line of your headline instead of the shorter headline in larger ads. The long headline can be up to 90 characters and may or may not appear with the description.
- DESCRIPTION – Up to 5. Descriptions have a maximum of 90 characters.
- BUSINESS NAME – Up to 25 characters.

Once you complete all required fields, Google will display samples of how your ad will appear for various sizes using a variety of images, headlines and descriptions that you provided

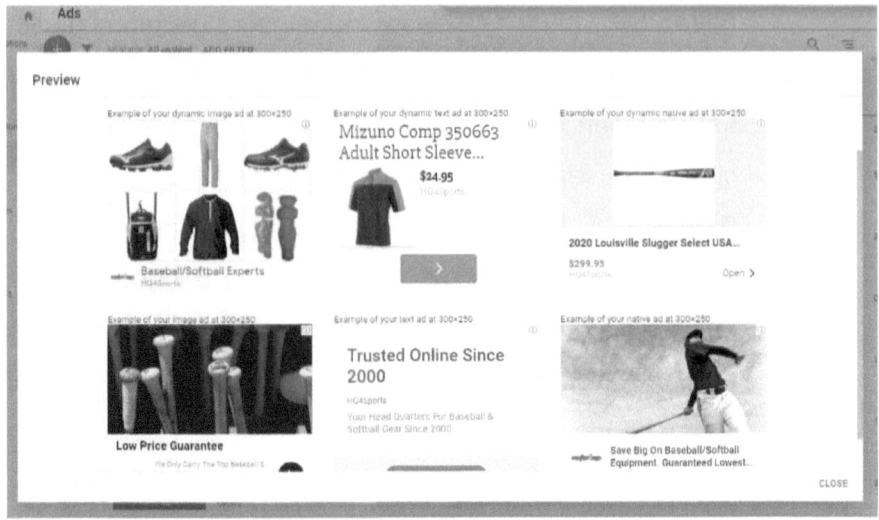

Dynamic Responsive Display Ads

In addition, advertisers have the ability to enhance their responsive display ads by connecting a product data feed. When you connect your product data feed, your responsive display ads become dynamic responsive display ads.

When a data feed from Google Merchant Center is linked to an ad, the actual product images will appear in the ad that the user visited while on your website.

Because ads are displayed in different sizes, products may not always appear, so it will be important to add a main URL link to where you would like someone to be directed if they click on your dynamic responsive display ad.

In addition, Google may show automatic tags on the products in your ads based on historical data of products within your data feed. These tags can include 'hot' or 'price drop' or 'new'. Unfortunately, advertisers have no control over these tags. Google automatically will insert these tags based on product insights from your linked feed.

For complete directions on how to set up and link a data feed from Google Merchant Center to Google Ads, review Chapter 3: *Linking Your Remarketing Campaign With Your Data Feed.*

Final Word

By now, you should be well aware that, on average, 97% of visitors will leave your website without purchase. Retargeting allows advertisers to stay in front of these non-purchasers as they continue through the Google Display Network.

Responsive display ads allow advertisers to quickly create and start serving eye-catching, effective ads to those users in a variety of sizes that will seamlessly appear within the available ad space throughout the Google Display Network.

And although responsive display ads are easy to create, don't make the mistake that it will be easy to create effective ads.

In order to be effective, images need to be eye catching, and headlines need to be exciting and full of benefits. Think disruptive, and be aware that you will need to continue to test!

Chapter 6

Matching Audiences With Google Retargeting Ads

After you have linked your Google Analytics with your Google Ads account, created your audience(s) within Google Analytics, created your retargeting campaign, linked your campaign with your Merchant Center Data feed and created your Google retargeting ads, there is only one more step.

I told you it was simple.

Okay, maybe there are quite a few steps, but if done correctly, it will be worth it to be able to target the average 97% of users who first visit your website and do not purchase.

In fact, with regards to those 97%, that is our last step. The step consists of matching the audience that we created with our retargeting campaigns.

A Couple Things To Know

When matching your audience with Google retargeting, there are a couple of ways you can do this. You can match while creating your ad group or you can match after an ad group has already been created.

The ability to match audience with already created ad groups allows advertisers the ability to change audiences already within a previously created ad group.

The other important term to keep in mind when matching your audiences and campaigns is the difference between 'Targeting' and 'Observation.'

When you select an audience to be used with Targeting, ONLY members of that audience will be eligible to receive ads within the specified ad group.

When you select an audience to be used with Observation, then the selected audience, as well as any other eligible user, can be eligible to receive ads from an ad group.

Retargeting campaigns use the Targeting option. We created ads with the purpose of ONLY showing ads to a particular audience.

Using audience in Observation mode, in contrast, is typically used when adding audiences to search or shopping campaigns. Adding audiences to those type of campaigns allows an advertiser to increase a bid for users within a particular audience. Using Observation mode is also often a preferred option with traditional Google display ads.

Linking An Audience Within A New Campaign

We have already seen in Chapter 4 – *Creating A Retargeting Campaign* – that the first step is to select an audience.

However, as a refresher, here are the steps to select an audience created in Google Analytics when creating a new ad group.

1. Click on BROWSE
2. Select How they have interacted with your business (Remarketing and similar audiences).
3. Select Website visitors.
4. Select the audience or audiences that you wish to include within your ad group.

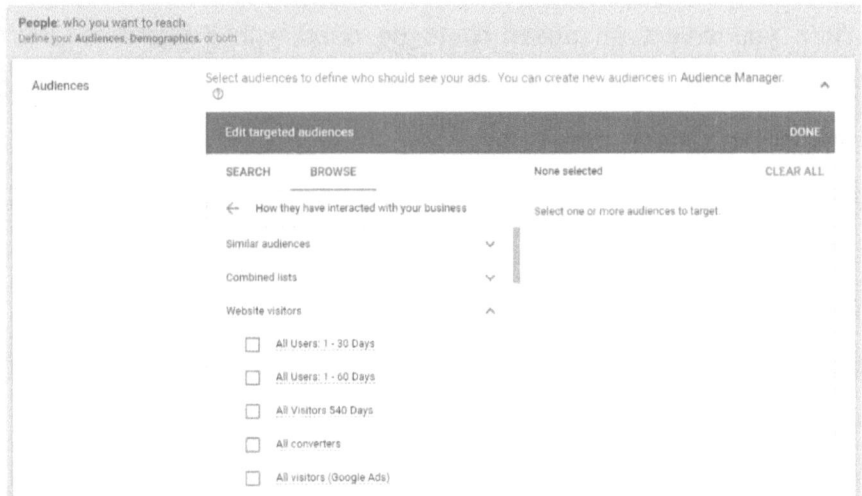

If you already have a created retargeting campaign, you may want to change the audience, add an audience or even remove an audience currently associated with a specific ad group.

Steps to modify or remove an audience in an existing ad group:

1. Navigate to the ad group.
2. Click on Audiences in the left-hand navigation menu.

3. To edit or remove an audience, you can check the box next to the audience and click the Edit button.

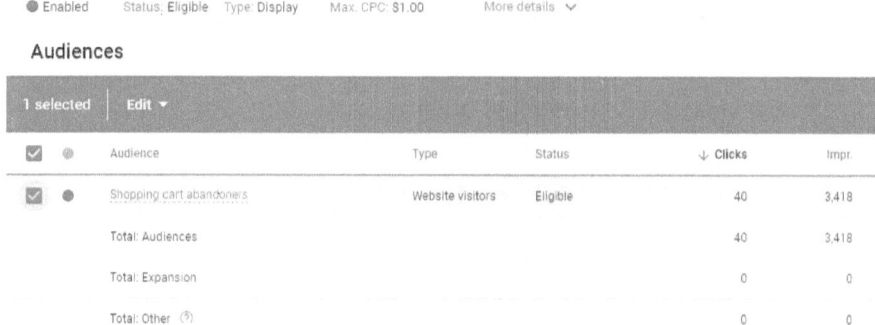

Steps to add an audience to an existing ad group:

1. Navigate to the ad group.
2. Click on Audiences in the left-hand navigation menu.
3. Click on the blue pencil icon
4. Click 'Edit Audiences,' and then it is just like adding an initial audience.
5. Click on BROWSE
6. Select How they have interacted with your business (Remarketing and similar audiences).
7. Select Website Visitors.

Being able to add, edit or remove an audience is convenient when working with multiple audiences within a Google ad group. However, keep in mind that currently you CANNOT have different bids for different audiences within the same ad group when the audiences are set to Targeting.

In order to be able to bid differently for different audiences, say product abandoners vs cart abandoners, you will need to add the audiences within separate ad groups.

Final Word

The final step before retargeting ads can begin serving, while simple, requires a bit of strategy in creating ad groups due to how you bid on the ads.

The strategy for creating audiences was already, or should have been already, performed when creating an audience.

Now it is time to put your strategy in place in terms of bidding.

What is the maximum amount that are you willing to pay based on the likelihood that a customer will make a purchase after being shown your retargeting ads?

That will be your bid. To calculate your bids, you may want to first review your past analytics and test. Remember that just because you set an initial bid does not mean it is set in stone.

Google is customizable, and the bids are easily changed. You want to make sure you are profitable with your bidding strategy, and this often takes testing and the creation of multiple ad groups containing different audiences.

Chapter 7

Opting Out of Google's Sneaky Target Expansion

By now, you may well be tired of me hammering home the fact that most visitors to your website are not going to buy. That is why we are creating retargeting campaigns. We want an effective way to reach the 97% of visitors that do not immediately buy.

It has also been shown that the more times a user visits your website, the more likely they are to ultimately make a purchase.

With that in mind, we have gone to great lengths to properly configure our audiences based on previous actions users have taken on our website. Our plan is to optimize our campaigns to serve our ads only to those who have previously visited our website.

However, pay attention, because this is where Google has recently gotten sneaky!

Google is now automatically opting your retargeting campaigns into what they term 'Targeting expansion.'

What targeting expansion does is show your retargeting ads to users 'similar' to the users within audiences that you created.

Google does not share the algorithm they use to decide how 'similar' users are, just that they are similar. Users Google deems as similar have never visited your website, they have just been deemed as similar to users who have.

Google also provides a sliding bar where you can decrease the level of similarity to include even more users who are even less similar to your created audience. Target expansion is designed to add a greater number of users to those to whom your retargeting ads will be eligible to appear.

This is all new.

With retargeting, we are advertising to users when they are doing something other than actively shopping for our products.

The nature of this alone makes conversion substantially less than those visitors on your website who find your website while shopping online. Now, Google is including users who have most likely never heard of you or your website.

How do you think that will go?

Before Google added target expansion, when creating a remarketing campaign, advertisers would know that they were only retargeting to their audience defined as those that previously visited their website.

With the feature of target expansion, advertisers automatically are opted in to serving ads to those that previously visited their website that are included in a selected audience as well as those deemed 'similar.'

And the sneaky thing?

Most advertisers do not realize it, as the setting for target expansion is well-hidden within the more ad group settings area of the Google Ads interface.

What I have found with private clients is that, without fail, target expansion will substantially increase spend without increasing your conversions.

This, of course, makes sense because those users in target expansion have never been to your website and most likely don't even know who you are.

Below, you will find steps on how you opt out of Targeting expansion while creating new campaigns as well as opting out of Targeting expansion with existing campaigns.

Opting Out While Creating A New Retargeting Campaign

Creating a dynamic remarketing campaign will allow you, the advertiser, to show your products within an ad to users who viewed your website throughout the Google Display Network.

Here again are the steps:

1. Click Campaigns from the page menu.
2. Click the plus button to create a new campaign.
3. In the "Goals" section, choose 'Sales.'
4. From the "Campaign type" section, select Display Network.
5. Select 'Standard display campaign.'
6. Enter your business website URL.
7. Next, you'll set parameters for your campaign, including:
    - Campaign name

- Location and language settings
- Bid strategy and budget

8. Click Additional settings for more options, like ad scheduling, content exclusions, or device targeting (This is where you will have wanted to link a data feed in order to show dynamic ads, see image below). Note, in order to connect a data feed, you must have already linked your Google Ads Account with your Google Merchant Center Account as described back in Chapter 3.

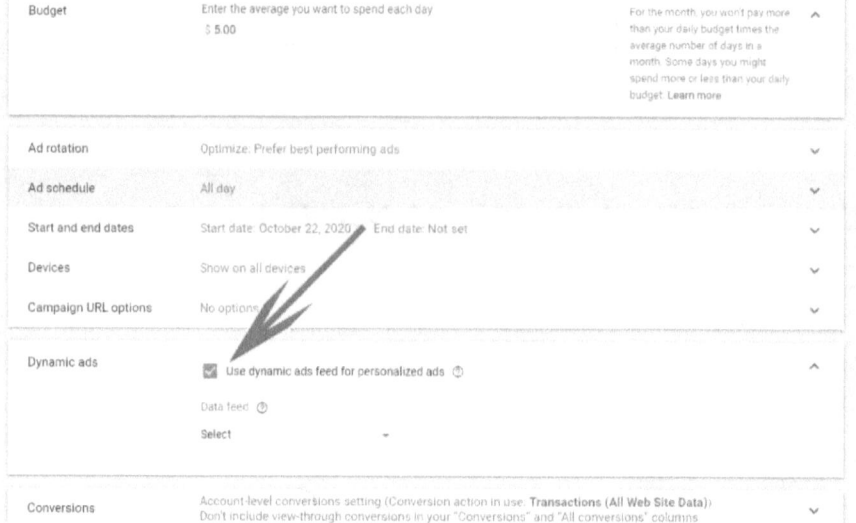

9. Next, look for "Audiences" in the "People" section. To serve ads to visitors who have visited your website and left, you will need to use a custom audience that you create in Google Analytics as described in Chapter 2.

Click Remarketing. To select an already prepared audience, click 'Browse' and then 'How they have interacted with your business.'

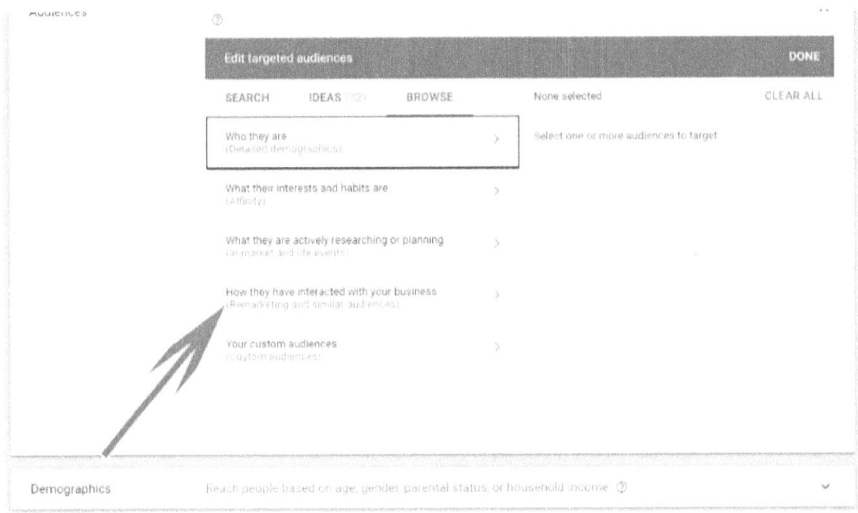

10. Click the checkbox next to the audiences that you would like to add. This will add them to your targeting.
11. Below the audience, you will see the 'Targeting expansion.' This is where Google will automatically opt you in to showing your ads to users 'similar' to your audience. In order to opt out, slide the slider to the off position.

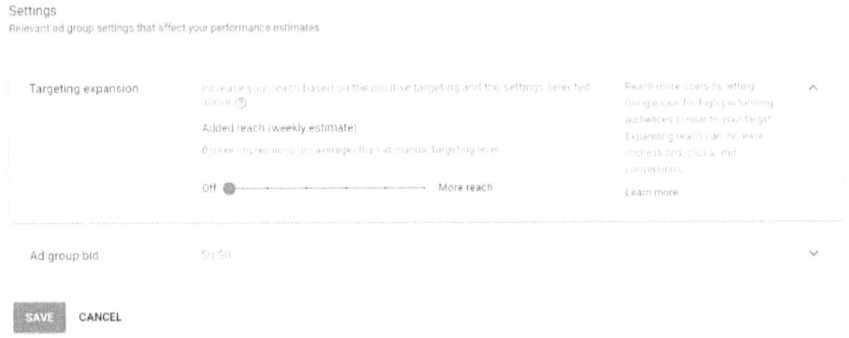

12. Create your Ad group bid.
13. Create your Ad.
14. Click the 'Create Campaign' button.

Forgetting To Turn Off The Target Expansion

If you follow the steps above, your dynamic retargeting ads will be correctly configured, and you will start to serve your ads only to previous website visitors that you have identified within a selected audience.

However, what if you forget to take one of these steps? Even worse, what if you see an unexplained spike in traffic and spend in your new retargeting campaign?

If you see more traffic than you are expecting, chances are that you either used a wrong audience with the campaign or forgot to turn off 'Targeting Expansion.'

Fortunately, you can adjust your campaign settings even after the campaign has been created.

Here are the steps:

1. Click Campaigns from the page menu.
2. Select your newly created retargeting campaign.
3. Click on the Ad Group that you want to adjust.
4. Click Settings from the left-hand navigation menu.
5. Click on the 'Edit ad group targeting' button.

6. Once you click on the 'Edit ad group targeting' button, then you can scroll down and toggle the Targeting Expansion to Off.

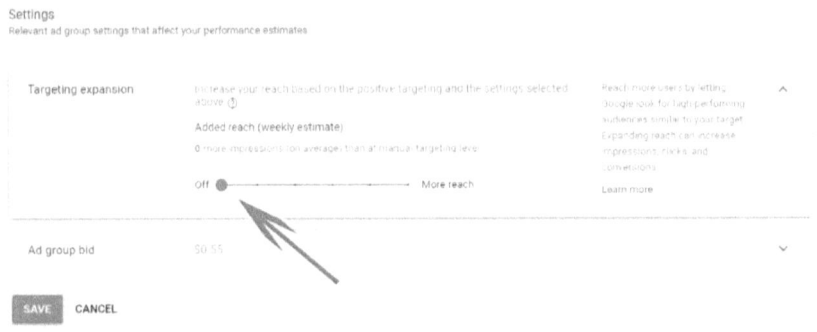

Quick note, to adjust and turn off Targeting Expansion once a campaign is created, it must be done from the Ad Group Settings not the Campaign Settings. In addition, it must be done on EVERY ad group where you wish to opt-out of Targeting Expansions.

I told you. How sneaky is that?

Not only does Google automatically opt-in campaigns to Targeting Expansion, but they burry the option to adjust it including the ability to opt out under the Ad Group Setting.

Final Word

Retargeting is a fantastic way to stay in front of the 97% of users who leave your website without purchasing.

Just like with Shopping and Search Ads, with Retargeting ads, you don't pay unless a user clicks on your ad. This means that if a user sees your ads reminding them of your product or service and simply goes and types in your website URL, well, you don't pay.

In addition, by using audiences, you can determine how much you ultimately are willing to pay for one type of website abandoner vs another.

Example, I always set bids higher for those users who reached the cart page and leave the website versus those that leave a product page before adding a product to their shopping cart.

If you recall, by using your product feed and cookies, you can show a user the exact product that they were looking at on your website within the retargeting ad that you later serve them.

All this works very well. However, what I've found doesn't work well is when Google tacks on similar users.

By opting campaigns into Targeting Expansion, it will likely lower your profitability and significantly increase your spend.

And worse than that?

It is just plain sneaky!!

Chapter 8

Limiting Locations Where Ads Can Appear

By now, you should be keenly aware that our retargeting ads, once created and approved, are going to be eligible to appear within the Google Display Network (GDN).

You also should know that, by default, Google will opt in to displaying our retargeting ads across EVERY eligible location within the Google Display Network.

Therefore, for our ads to be as effective as possible, we need to fully understand what the Google Display Network includes and where, or even more importantly, where it does not make sense for our ads to appear.

The GDN is a collection of websites that includes Google-owned websites such as YouTube, Gmail, Google Finance, Blogger as well as thousands of other non-Google sites, mobile sites and apps.

The Google-owned sites of YouTube, Gmail Google Finance, and Blogger, everyone knows, and they typically perform well for retargeting. Having your ads appear within these sites should not be the cause of excess ad spend or any other negative issues that may come along with other type sites (as we will soon detail). However, even though they have historically performed well for other advertisers, it is still prudent to keep an eye on your own performance for these sites once your ads begin to serve.

Now the 'thousands of other non-Google sites' is a bit of a mystery. Since 2003, Google has a run a program named Google AdSense. Google AdSense is a cross platform application where websites can opt in to allowing Google display ads and receive direct payment from Google based on how many users visit their website.

Almost 20 years-old, Google AdSense was introduced as a method Google effectively used to exponentially increase their reach across the internet. In fact, many websites over the years have been created for the sole purpose of serving Google Ads, although the practice of doing so is not quite as common as a few years back. If you ever clicked on a listing to discover a page with just Google ads and links, this is an example of one of those websites.

Today, most of the websites included in the 'thousands of other non-Google sites' within the Google GDN are legitimate websites that are not only available to Google Ads but ads from other retargeting companies as well.

From ESPN to branded news sites, the list of websites that are included are too many to list. Overall, the 'other non-Google sites' typically perform well for retargeting ads, but again, your performance will still need monitoring on a continued basis as we will cover in the upcoming chapter.

Finally, there are the mobile sites and apps. This is where an account typically will suffer quite a bit of waste with retargeting ad spend.

By now, most of us are aware of what a mobile app is, but to be clear for those that may not, a mobile app is a software application designed specifically to run on a mobile device.

Here, hence, lies part of the problem. Typically, we find that mobile devices have quite a bit lower conversion rate than desktop devices. Add this fact to trying to target users who are on their phones with the purpose of visiting a mobile app, and it is no wonder that showing retargeting ads for mobile apps typically is a waste of advertising dollars.

Second and just as important, Google Play, another mobile app option, currently lacks the security of Apple Apps. This lack of security fosters the possibility of click fraud, or non-valid clicks, costing ad dollars. There has been quite the number of case studies released showing click fraud involved with ads appearing on apps, especially with Google Play Apps.

Third are unattended clicks. Whether it is a user confusing your ad as part of whatever candy crush game they are playing or little Johnny accidentally pushing buttons on the app his mother gave him to occupy his time, there is no doubt that unattended clicks are also an issue advertising on mobile apps.

You can do the math and even test running your ads on mobile apps, but these three reasons are why I almost always recommend opting out of serving retargeting ads on mobile apps when first creating a retargeting campaign.

LIMITING LOCATIONS WHERE ADS CAN APPEAR

Previously, Google made it fairly straightforward to remove ads from appearing from mobile apps. All that an advertiser needed to do was add 'Adsenseformobileapps.com' to your Placement exclusions and none of your Google Display Ads including retargeting ads would appear on mobile apps.

Unfortunately for advertisers, this no longer works.

Currently, it is much more difficult to remove being shown on mobile apps and almost impossible to remove 100% from mobile apps.

However, the reasons above not to be listed make it still well worth the effort. The steps below, along with the upcoming chapter, list the most up-to-date strategies on opting out of mobile apps for display ads in specifically retargeting campaigns.

Excluding Ads From Appearing on Mobile Apps:

1. Login to your campaign.
2. Click on Placements in the left-hand menu, then Exclusions. Here you will see any current exclusions for the campaign.
3. To add new exclusions, click on the blue pencil icon.
4. You will have two options: 'Exclude placements' and 'Edit ad group targeting'

You can exclude mobile placements with either option; however, I prefer using the 'Exclude placements' option. When excluding a mobile app, you will need to individually click on each app you wish to exclude. Therefore, when running multiple retargeting campaigns, I will first create a placement exclusion list and use this list to quickly exclude all mobile apps (instructions below).

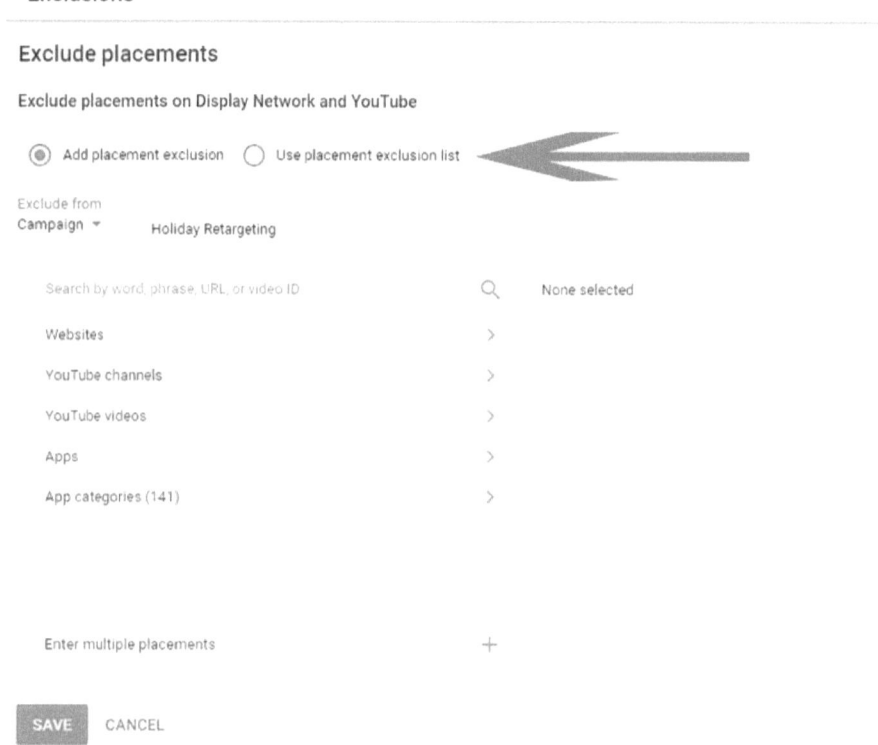

5. Select the placement exclusions or use a placement exclusion list (instructions below) and save.

You will see a screen that displays the list of all your excluded locations.

Exclusions		
Network: Display ADD FILTER		
Exclusion ↑	Type	Exclude
All Apps > Google Play > Art & Design	Mobile application category	Holiday
All Apps > Google Play > Auto & Vehicles	Mobile application category	Holiday
All Apps > Google Play > Beauty	Mobile application category	Holiday
All Apps > Apple App Store > Book	Mobile application category	Holiday
All Apps > Google Play > Books & Reference	Mobile application category	Holiday
All Apps > Google Play > Business	Mobile application category	Holiday
All Apps > Apple App Store > Business	Mobile application category	Holiday
All Apps > Apple App Store > Catalogs	Mobile application category	Holiday
All Apps > Google Play > Comics	Mobile application category	Holiday
All Apps > Google Play > Communication	Mobile application category	Holiday
All Apps > Google Play > Dating	Mobile application category	Holiday
All Apps > Google Play > Education	Mobile application category	Holiday

If you have multiple campaigns, instead of adding all exclusions manually, you may find it more efficient to create a placement exclusion list.

Once created, you can easily apply your placement exclusion list at the campaign level or apply the list to multiple campaigns through the Shared Library.

Creating A Placement Exclusion List

1. Click on Tools & Settings (wrench icon in top navigation bar).
2. Click on Placement exclusion lists under Shared Library.

MAKE EACH CLICK COUNT USING GOOGLE RETARGETING

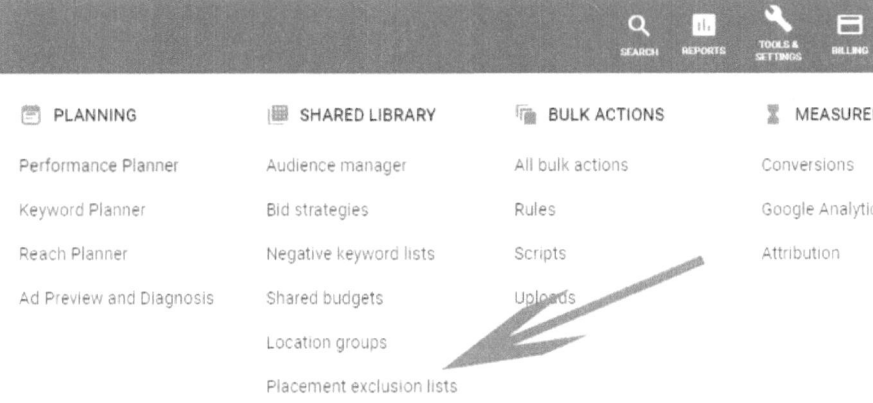

3. Click on the blue plus button to create a new placement exclusion list.
4. Name your list and select your exclusions one-by-one, just like you would do for an individual campaign, and Save.
5. While in the Share Library, you can assign this new list to specific campaigns by clicking on the Apply to Campaigns button.

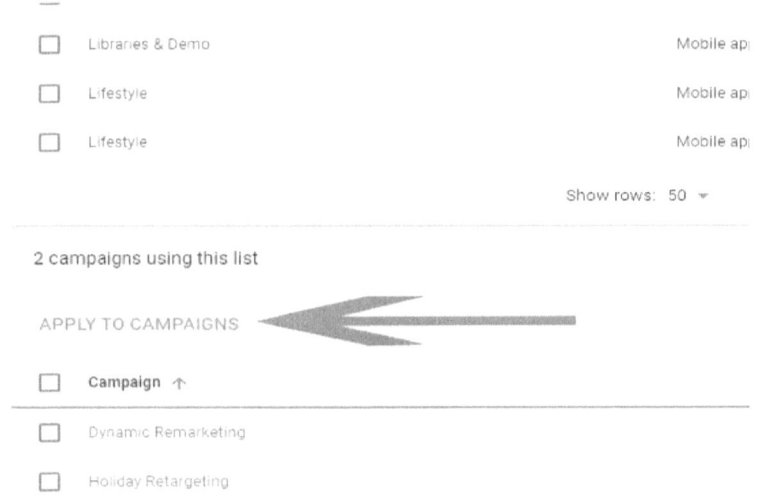

6. Once you click this button, a window will appear displaying eligible display campaigns. Select the campaigns for which you wish to apply the list and click Done.
7. Google will then display which campaigns are using your new placement exclusion list.

As previously noted, once you have a placement exclusion list created, you can also apply the list within the 'Exclude placements' campaign settings.

Either way you decide to exclude mobile apps, it is important to make sure it is done. By limited serving ads on mobile apps, most advertisers will find their retargeting campaigns substantially more successful.

Excluding Ads From Appearing Based On Content

Now that we have excluded mobile apps, many times it is also recommended that you exclude appearing for some content.

Excluding content isn't as much about increasing your results as it is about protecting your brand.

Let me explain.

Do you want your retargeting ads appearing on a news site reporting a tragic event? Do you want your retargeting ads appearing on a website with adult content?

It probably depends on what you are selling, but for many advertisers, the would answer will be no.

Excluding specific content can only be done at the account level. In order to exclude ads from appearing for certain content, follow these steps:

Excluding Sensitive Content:

1. From the left-hand navigation menu, click on 'All Campaigns' view.
2. Click on Settings from the left-hand page menu, then 'Account settings.'
3. Click on Excluded Content. Note, the default is to show ads on all content.

LIMITING LOCATIONS WHERE ADS CAN APPEAR

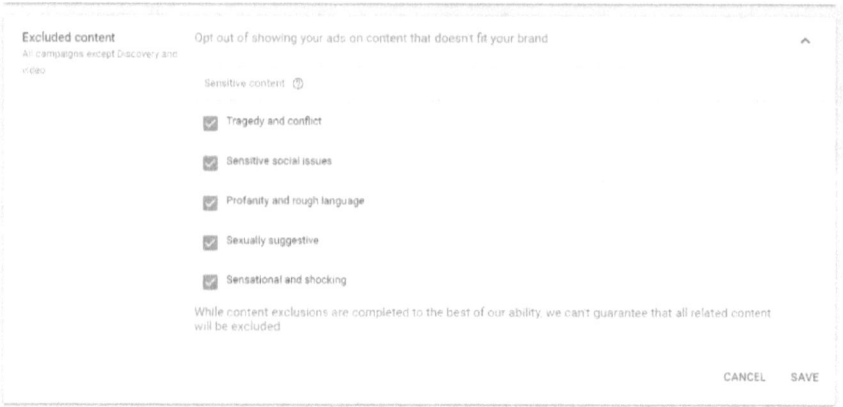

4. Select the type of sensitive content that you do not want your ads to appear on and save. Your options are Tragedy and conflict, Sensitive social issues, Profanity and rough language, Sexually suggestive and Sensational and shocking. Note, For the majority of my private clients, I opt out of all.

Here is how Google defines each category –

- Sensitive content - Tragedy and conflict: Excludes graphic content of combat or war.
- Sensitive social issues: Excludes content intended to elicit a response about controversial issues.
- Profanity and rough language: Excludes content with infrequent or mild profanity, or profanity used in entertainment, comedy, satire, or music.
- Sexually suggestive content: Excludes content about sex or sexual products.
- Sensational and shocking: Excludes content of disasters or accidents that show casualties or death.

- Once you save, you will see the excluded content listed in the main account settings.

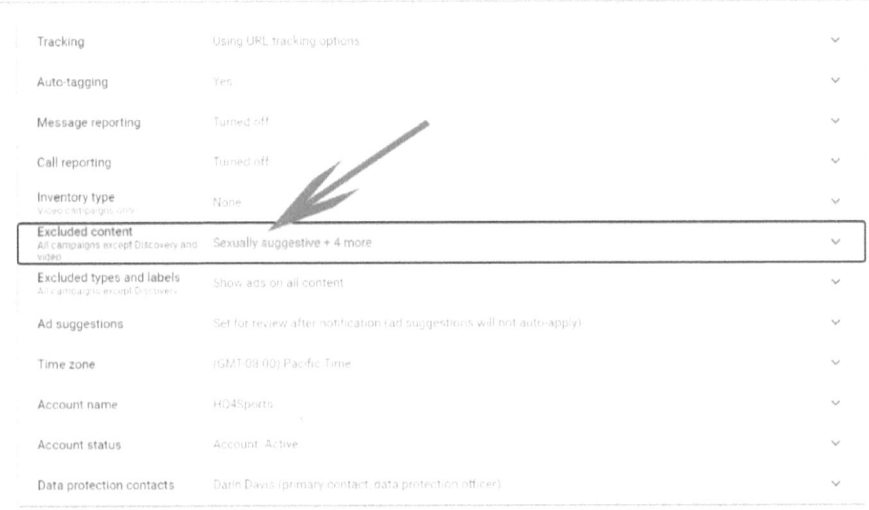

Excluding Types and Labels

In addition to excluding sensitive content, which I typically will suggest, advertisers also can exclude serving display ads on other types of content that may not fit their brand image.

To exclude other content, follow the same basic steps, but select 'Exclude types and labels.'

1. From the left-hand navigation menu, click on 'All Campaigns' view.
2. Click on Settings from the left-hand page menu, then 'Account settings.'
3. Click on 'Exclude types and labels.' Note, the default is to show ads on all types and labels.
4. To exclude, check the boxes where you DO NOT wish for your ads to be eligible to appear.

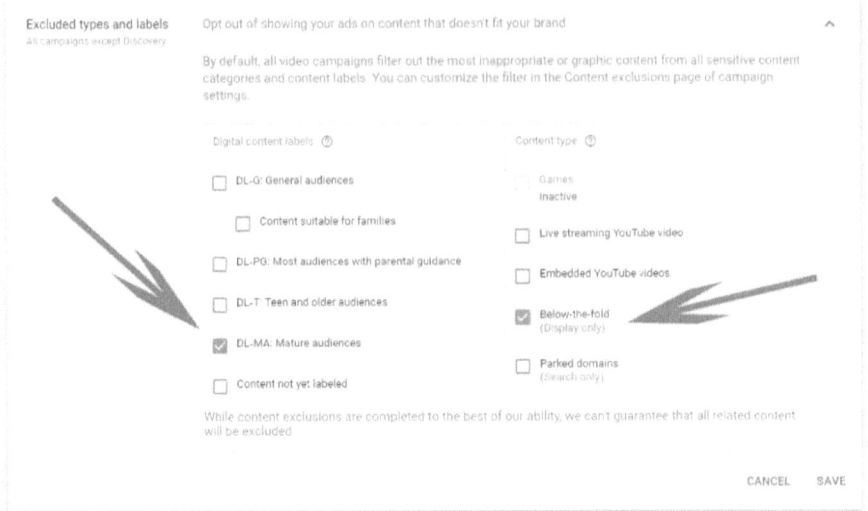

Note, where you want to exclude your ads from appearing will depend on your brand and your advertising goals, but typically, I will opt out of serving ads to Mature audiences as well as serving ads 'Below the fold.'

Final Word

Very few things work as well as they could 'out of the box.' Your retargeting advertising settings are no exception.

By being able to exclude your ads based on content as well as by content type, you can effectively control where your ads will appear.

By utilizing these settings properly, we can ensure that our products are not displayed for content which is not congruent with our brand.

These settings are just the tip of the iceberg. Next chapter, we will dive into looking at specific results for the placements that are eligible to display our retargeting ads including how to exclude individual mobile app placements.

For now, remember, the goal of retargeting ads is to drive our previous website users back to our website. You should not risk having ads appear on pages with sensitive content. Do yourself a favor and leave the sensitive and shocking content to your competitors and protect your brand image.

We all, as profit obsessed advertisers, would like an easier way to exclude mobile apps and excluding our ads appearing on sensitive content. However, Google has certainly made it a bit more difficult than it previously was.

Being difficult is not necessarily a bad thing. Being more difficult most likely means that your competitors are not doing the work, which is good news for us.

We will happily let our competitors spend their ad dollars on appearing on mobile apps and soiling their brand name by appearing alongside sensitive content. For us, we will do the work to keep our brand clean and our ad dollars spent wisely.

Chapter 9

Targeting Where Your Ads Appear

Now that we have limited where our ads are eligible to appear, in this chapter, we shift our focus to targeting optimal locations.

We have seen how much budget it will use and how difficult it is to opt out of serving our retargeting ads on mobile apps.

However, beyond traditional websites, there is another placement that has done extraordinarily well for my private clients' retargeting ads.

That placement is YouTube Ads channels of related products.

What do I mean related products?

I'll give you a few examples.

For my private client who sells baseball gear, I target placements serving his retargeting ads on specific baseball related YouTube channels.

For my private client who sells pond fountains, I target placements serving his retargeting ads on pond related fountains.

Why does advertising on related YouTube channels typically perform well?

It has to do with browser intent. When a user visits a mobile app, their intent is to interact with the mobile app. Therefore, mobile apps typically have poor performance.

When a user visits a YouTube video, their intent is to learn and discover more about the subject of the YouTube video.

Learning is just below the intent threshold of buying, and that is why advertising on YouTube videos typically has positive results for retargeting ads.

With retargeting ads, wouldn't my clients' retargeting ads appear anyway for subject matter related YouTube videos, you may be asking?

The answer is yes.

Retargeting ads would be absolutely be eligible to appear. However, the reason I recommend adding additional placements is two-fold:

First, by targeting high volume YouTube channels, advertisers can substantially increase their bidding on specific channels, thus increasing the likelihood and frequency of appearing on these YouTube channels.

Second, once you can determine which YouTube channel performs well for your retargeting ads, you have the option to apply that knowledge to create ads on those YouTube channels for visitors who have not visited your website (aka display ads).

We will not discuss display ads in detail; however, using YouTube ads with text ads, or even better, with your own YouTube videos is the most effective way that I have found to successfully advertise using pure display ads.

Adding YouTube Channels Placements:

To add specific YouTube channels, follow these instructions:

1. Click on the Placements drop down in the left-hand navigation and then on Placements sub-category.
2. Click the blue pencil icon and select 'Edit Placements.'

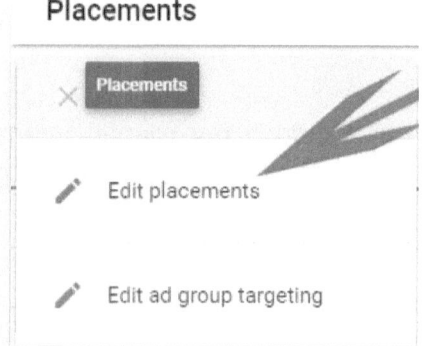

3. Select which ad group you would like to add the placements. (Note, selecting placements is done at the ad group level).
4. Select Targeting or Observation. This is a critical distinction. If you pick Targeting, your ads in the selected ad group will ONLY be eligible to appear for those destinations. Observation will continue to allow ads to appear everywhere, but you can increase the bids on selected placements, which will be our goal. Therefore, it is recommended to select observation

Edit placements

Choose placements to show ads on specific websites, apps, or videos

Dynamic Remarketing > New Visitors 1 - 30 Days

○ Targeting (recommended)
Narrow the reach of your ad group to the selected audiences, with the option to adjust the bids

◉ Observation ⓘ
Don't narrow the reach of your ad group, with the option to adjust the bids on the selected audiences

5. The next step is to select where you wish to add the observation. For now, we are going to look at adding related YouTube channels; however, note that you can also add specific YouTube videos, Websites, Apps or even App categories.

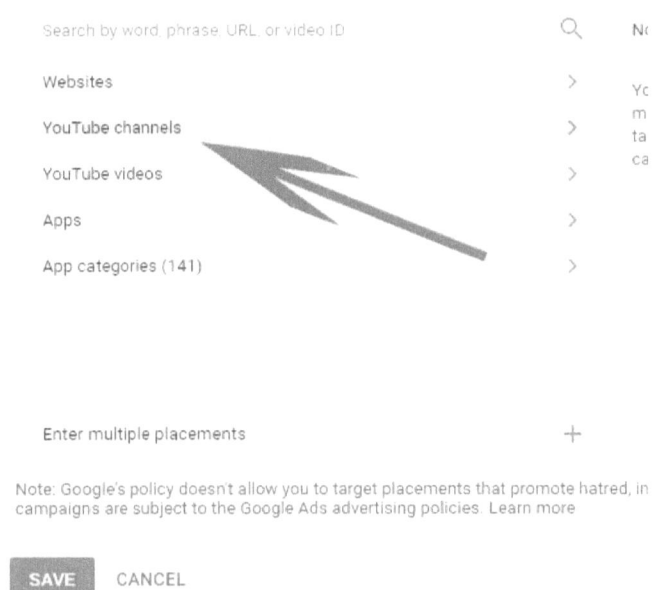

6. After you click on YouTube channels, you can use the search to find related channels. Note, in the example below, I use the search term baseball; however, for your purpose, use what is relevant for your business.
7. Select the related YouTube videos and save.

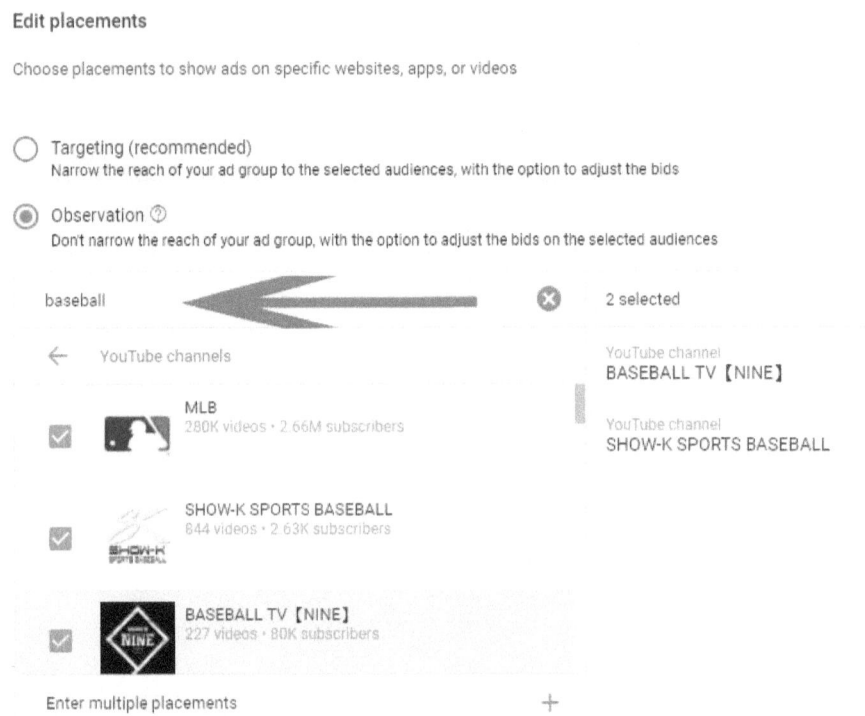

8. Now, in order to adjust the bids for those placements, you will check the boxes next to the desired placements; select Edit and Change bid adjustments.

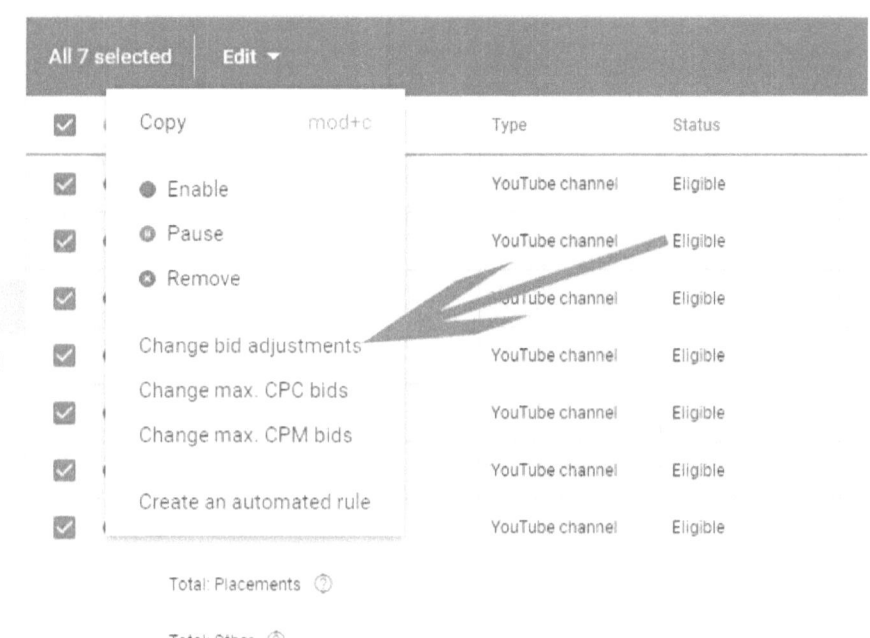

9. Finally, select how much you want to increase your bids. Since by nature, using retargeting has limited reach, here I am extremely aggressive with my bids. Notice in the example below, I have the bid increased by 500%! Remember, you won't be charged unless the ad is clicked, but I want to make sure for past visitors that I give my ad the best possible chance to appear.

TARGETING WHERE YOUR ADS APPEAR

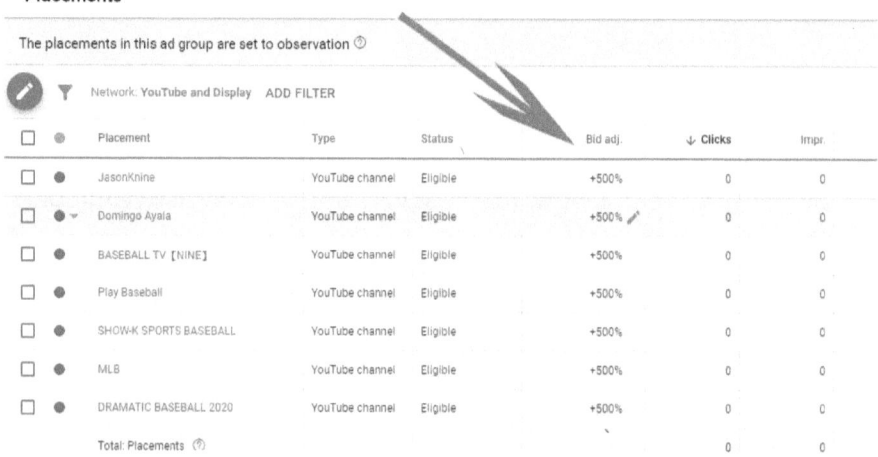

10. Click on the Apply button, and you are done.

Final Word

Increasing the bids on specific YouTube channels is an advanced strategy where a sizable audience list is needed to realize any substantial traffic.

Additionally, beyond a large audience you are targeting, how many followers a YouTube channel has along with how many YouTube channels you are targeting will determine your traffic levels.

Also, it is bolded and emphasized in the steps above, but it is critical when setting up this technique that you understand the difference between the targeting and the observation modes.

The Targeting mode 'targets' only select placements while the Observation mode 'observes' all eligible placement, specifically reporting 'observing' select placements.

The strategy shown in this chapter details how to use retargeting ads to advertise effectively on specific product-related YouTube channels.

However, as advertisers, you can absolutely use this technique to effectively serve other ads targeting product-specific YouTube channels for display advertising using both text and your own YouTube video ads.

Targeting YouTube ads is a newer feature in the Google platform, meaning less competition and more potential for advertisers who implement a correct strategy.

Chapter 10

Frequency – Controlling How Often Your Retargeting Ads Are Shown

The term frequency refers to how often your retargeting ads appear, or more accurately, the maximum number of times ads are eligible to appear to users.

By now, anyone who has spent considerable time on their screens are keenly aware of retargeting ads. Very few people anymore think that it is coincidence that the new toaster they were looking at last week is now being shown within an ad in our Gmail account purely by coincidence.

However, there is still a fine line between subtly nudging a user to return to your website by showing your ads occasionally and repeatedly blasting them your ad 20 times per day, every day so everywhere they look, they see that proverbial toaster.

A question commonly asked is how does an advertiser determine how often (the frequency) to serve retargeting ads to their customers?

However, before we can ask how often, we must ask if we, as advertisers, have the ability to control the frequency.

The answer to this is yes.

With a remarketing campaign, we have two choices.

1. Let Google determine the frequency.
2. Manually set the frequency.

Google Determining the Frequency

The easiest and most convenient way to control frequency is to let Google decide how often to serve your ads. After all, Google knows everything, right?

If you have read through my previous books or listened to many of my Podcast episodes in the past, you probably already know what I'm going to say.

I believe that Google is perhaps the most perfect advertising channel ever built because they provide advertisers with the ability to reach shoppers while they are shopping. However, I don't believe much in Google's automated bidding strategies or even with their formulas on frequency.

My belief is that an advertiser, in tune with their own product line, will be much more effective determining their frequency based on their audiences, time of year and, of course, their own testing rather than relying on Google's algorithm.

Manually Set The Frequency

What would be the reason to manually set the frequency, you may be asking. There are a few situations when I recommend manually setting the frequency, and we will look at a couple of examples before we look at directions for how to do it.

Busy shopping times. For eCommerce companies, this could be the holiday shopping season. As we approach the holidays, Black Friday week to be specific, shopping online becomes fast and furious and is a great example of when you may consider increasing your frequency settings.

For these times when customers are likely to make a buying decision quickly, you don't want to lose a sale for a shopper who be visiting many websites looking for gifts for a brother, sister, parents and kids. Therefore, I typically will turn up frequency on high buyer intent audiences such as 'Shopping Cart Abandoners.'

In contrast, slow periods of the year are a time when you may consider reducing your frequency. An example of this would be a private client I have who sells pond fountains.

Typically, in the winter months, particularly in states where outdoor ponds freeze over, not many people are thinking of installing a $3,000 fountain. Therefore, it makes sense to decrease the frequency of retargeting ads.

Hopefully, these examples have gotten the wheels in your head spinning on what may make sense for your business. However, like anything, I always recommend testing to discover what is the most profitable for your company.

Note that the frequency capping is available only at the Campaign level and not at specific ad group levels. Therefore, if for some reason you wish to have different frequency capping for different ad groups, then they will need to be placed within different campaigns. Also, you should note that, currently, advertisers can only modify the frequency of ads within an already existing campaign. Therefore, once you have created a campaign, here are the instructions on changing how often your ads are eligible to be shown to your selected audience.

Changing The Frequency Setting on an Existing Campaign:

1. Login to your Google Ads Account
2. Select All campaigns in the navigation panel.
3. Click the campaign you wish to edit.
4. Select Settings in the left-hand menu.
5. Click Additional settings.
6. Select Frequency Management.
7. Set your preference. You have the ability to manage your impressions by ad, ad group or whole campaign.
8. Click save.

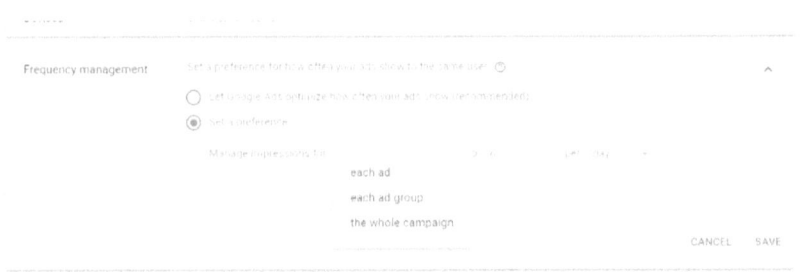

Final Word

How many is the appropriate number of times that a retargeting ad should be served to a someone who previously visited your website and for how long should ads be served?

These are key questions that vary from website to website, but I believe that the answer typically will vary.

To determine what is most effective for your website, you will need to test.

However, fortunately, given the steps in this chapter, you can test how many times retargeting ads will be shown.

In order to address how long ads will be shown (the number of days between when a user visits your website and when they are no longer eligible to be shown your retargeting ads), you will need to adjust your audience.

Websites will vary on what is the optimal setting, but here are my frequent recommendations when first starting to test different settings with my private clients:

- Change the length of duration on the audience from Google's standard 30 days to 60 days.
- Manage impressions for each ad group to 6 per day.
- Increase this number to 12 per day during busy seasons.
- Decrease this number to 2 per day during slow seasons.

Like with most settings within the Google's Ad interface, you will want to test and track to discover where your highest profitability will be generated.

Chapter 11

Adjusting Bids Based On Device

One of the most effective ways to optimize your retargeting campaigns is by managing the number of clicks generated from mobile vs. tablets vs. desktop users.

With normal Google search ads as well as Google shopping ads, most advertisers discover that traffic from mobile devices typically does not convert nearly as well as traffic from the other two types of devices.

Even for the most mobile friendly websites, mobile conversion is, on average, about half of that of desktop devices and 30% to 40% less than conversion rates from tablets.

Given that we know mobile is not going to perform as well with conversion rates, it probably does not make sense to bid the same across all devices, or does it?

The answer to this question is going to come down to your purpose in using retargeting and with your budget.

If your budget is unlimited and your goal is to continue to get your website in front of as many eyeballs of past visitors as possible, then perhaps leaving your bidding the same for all devices makes sense.

However, if you are confined by a marketing budget or you are looking to squeeze the most out of your marketing dollars, then it will make sense to bid lower on mobile devices and higher on desktop and tablets.

In this chapter, we are going to look at how to optimize bids based on device and optimize bids based on your specific campaign history.

Optimizing Bids By Device

Why do mobile devices typically not perform as well as desktop devices?

To answer that question, think about the users' intent with mobile devices.

Hopefully, it comes as no shock to you that more people are visiting your website from their iPhones than from their desktop devices (which includes laptops).

I am comfortable safely making that statement, because according to Google, mobile traffic first exceeded desktop traffic back in 2016. Since then, the percentage of mobile traffic has continued to increase every year, with the hiccup of 2020, where the percentage of mobile usage slightly decreased.

Even in 2020, research has shown that the average person spends an almost unimaginable 3 hours on their phone per day, and according to data compiled by Bankmycell, on average, users will check their phones an astonishing 63 times per day!

This makes it important to realize what activities people are performing on their smart phones.

The top 5 activities performed on mobile devices include:

1. Messaging
2. Social media
3. Web Browsing
4. Email
5. Camera

You may have noticed that actively searching for your product or website did not make the list!

You might think that all these statistics are meaningless; after all, if a past website visitor is shown your ad and clicks on your retargeting ads, they must be interested in your product.

To a degree, this is correct; however, especially with a mobile device, it is difficult to gain and hold attention to your products or website. In addition, many times, those clicks are erroneous as users rely on their fingers to navigate small screens.

Regardless of which device they are using or even the reason they visit your website, it is important to know your specific numbers, especially when it comes to conversion.

Know Your Mobile Numbers

Statistics are helpful, but the real question becomes what is the appropriate bidding strategy for mobile devices for your company?

The answer depends on your specific company and can be determined in part based on your answers to the following questions:

1. What percentage of your traffic comes from mobile?
2. What is your conversion rate on mobile visitors?
3. Is your site optimized for mobile (how does it look for mobile users)?
4. How are your current campaigns working for mobile including your current ROI and ROAS (how profitable are they)?

These are fundamental questions that each marketer needs to know the answer to in order to begin optimizing their paid advertising for mobile.

Fortunately, by having Google Analytics installed along with the historical data available from your Google Ads account, the answers to these questions can be easily attained.

Answering The Questions

The first two questions of what percentage of your traffic is generated from mobile devices along with the conversion rates generated from mobile visitors can be answered at the same time.

To view an overview of your traffic, you will want to use Google Analytics. Later, when adjusting bids for individual campaigns, you will review historical data and adjust the bidding within the Google Ads interface.

The first step is to open your Google Analytics account. Hopefully, you already have Google Analytics properly installed as it provides much useful data for measuring the health of your overall website other than the conversions segmented by device.

In the left menu, select 'Audience' then 'Mobile' then 'Overview.' Here, you will be able to view your conversion rates based on device – mobile, desktop or tablet.

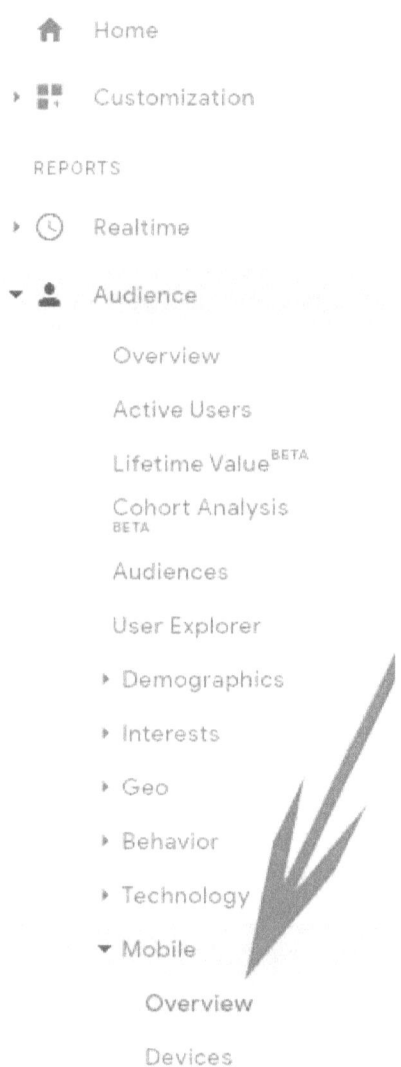

The numbers typically will appear as the example below:

ADJUSTING BIDS BASED ON DEVICE

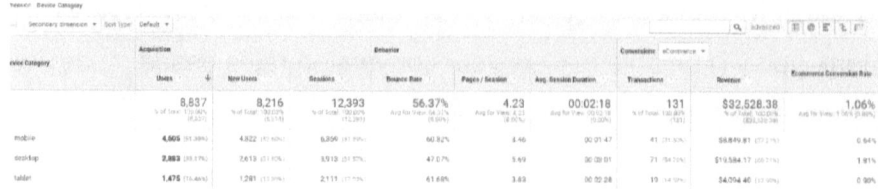

This is a very typical result for eCommerce retailers. It reveals that almost twice the traffic is coming from mobile devices (4,605 visits in mobile vs. 2,883 visits in desktop).

Looking at this report also reveals that the mobile conversion rate is only about 1/3 of that generated by desktop devices (0.64% - mobile vs 1.81% - desktop).

The report also shows statistics for tablets. Also, very typically in this example, tablets have about 1/2 the traffic of desktop, and the conversion rates are somewhere between mobile conversion rates and desktop conversion rates at 0.90%.

Now that we have answered the first two questions of what percentage of traffic is coming from mobile and what the conversion rates are for mobile devices, we can look at the question – is your site optimized for mobile?

There are different ways to optimize your website for mobile. In fact, Google offers free tools such as testing the speed of your website available through Google's developer tools

https://developers.google.com/speed/pagespeed/insights/ (which is very important).

However, I find that the most effective way to see if your website is optimized for mobile is to place test orders for your products using mobile devices. Put yourself through the user experience repeatedly

and you will discover if there are issues that could be lowering your conversion rates.

Ask your employees or family or friends to also test and give you honest feedback of anything they see that may prevent them from ordering using their iPhone or Android.

Today, almost everyone has experience online shopping, and you will find this type of feedback provides valuable and actionable insight.

I recommend personally placing orders using different devices at least every other week in order to deeply understand your website's checkout experience and to continue to troubleshoot any issues.

Although most mobile traffic comes from Apple iPhones, make sure you do not ignore other devices. To view which devices are generating traffic again, return to Google Analytics.

You are again going to go to the left navigation menu in Google Analytics and select 'Audience' then 'Mobile.' However, this time select 'Devices.' This report will display the traffic and conversion rates based on the different type of device – Apple iPhone, Tablet type, Samsung Android type, etc,

ADJUSTING BIDS BASED ON DEVICE

	Mobile Device Info	Acquisition	
Audiences		Users	New Users
User Explorer			
▶ Demographics		5,004	4,793
▶ Interests		% of Total: 23.97% (20,877)	% of Total: 24.35% (19,681)
▶ Geo			
▶ Behavior	1. Apple iPhone	2,275 (45.46%)	2,241 (46.76%)
▶ Technology	2. Apple iPad	1,040 (20.78%)	976 (20.36%)
▼ Mobile	3. Microsoft Windows RT Tablet	152 (3.04%)	133 (2.77%)
Overview	4. Samsung SM-G960U Galaxy S9	100 (2.00%)	95 (1.98%)
Devices	5. Samsung SM-G950U Galaxy S8	83 (1.66%)	82 (1.71%)
▶ Cross Device BETA	6. Samsung SM-G965U Galaxy S9+	70 (1.40%)	66 (1.38%)
▶ Custom	7. Samsung SM-G975U Galaxy S10+	70 (1.40%)	68 (1.42%)
Attribution BETA	8. Samsung SM-N960U Galaxy Note9	60 (1.20%)	54 (1.13%)
Discover	9. Samsung SM-G955U Galaxy S8+	48 (0.96%)	44 (0.92%)
Admin	10. Samsung SM-N950U Galaxy Note8	48 (0.96%)	48 (1.00%)

Lowering Bids on Mobile Devices

Once you gain a grasp on your website's historic conversion rates in regards to device and define your goal of using retargeting, then lowering device bids is relatively easy.

For simplicity, let us assume that you discovered your mobile conversion rate is half of your desktop conversion rates. Your goal is to maximize your ad spend within the confines of a budget, so you decide to lower your mobile bids by 50%.

Before we lower the bids, remember that limiting the number of mobile impressions and, more importantly, clicks is a two-step process. We have already reduced the number of clicks and impressions by limiting our presence on mobile apps. Now we can decrease the mobile clicks further by using bid adjustments.

Steps To Lower Bid Adjustments:

1. Navigate to your retargeting campaign.
2. In the left-hand navigation menu, select Devices.
3. Click on the bid adjustment column for the bid that you wish to adjust.

You can increase or decrease your bids in terms of percentage. Once you do, save and your bid adjustment is saved.

Devices					
Level: Campaign ADD FILTER					
Device	Level	Added to		Bid adj.	Ad gr
Mobile phones	Campaign	Dynamic Remarketing		-50%	4 ad
Computers	Campaign	Dynamic Remarketing		0%	4 ad
Tablets	Campaign	Dynamic Remarketing		-25%	1 ad
TV screens	Campaign	Dynamic Remarketing		0%	None
Total: Campa...					

It is important you realize how the bid adjustments work. If you are bidding $1 for instance, and decrease the bid by 50% for mobile devices, then your bid for mobile devices becomes $0.50.

Conversely, you can also increase your bid adjustments. If you are bidding $1 for instance, and increase the bid on desktop by 50%, then you would be bidding a maximum of $1.50 on desktop devices (computers).

Final Word

It is important to note that, typically, you will not see a large number of conversions generated through retargeting.

The actual number of conversions will, in part, depend on your conversion attribution settings. Whether you are counting conversions based on last click or by other means such as position-based goes a long way in determining the effectiveness of your retargeting (more on this in the next chapter).

Therefore, for those working with budget constraints, I recommend using historical data from your site through Google Analytics along with your campaign goals to make device bid adjustments.

Just because conversions may be lower than Shopping or Search ads does not mean that they should be non-existent with Retargeting campaigns.

It is important to test your ads as well as test your conversion process. Working on ways to increase your conversion rates on your website will work wonders in increasing conversion rates for both paid and organic traffic.

Chapter 12

Measuring the Success of Your Retargeting

Throughout this book, we have discussed ways to increase your effectiveness using retargeting ads.

The most common way to gauge the effectiveness of retargeting is to measure how much you spend compared to how much in revenue/sales your ads generate. Using these statistics, we can calculate our ROAS – Return on Ad Spend.

It is simple to calculate to determine ROAS: divide revenue generated by dollars spent.

A simple example. If a campaign spends $100 and generates $300 with a total of 5 conversions, your ROAS will be 3.

Calculation: 300 / 100 = 3.

With retargeting ads, even though the ROAS calculation is simple, getting to exactly how many conversions a retargeting ad is responsible for generating is a bit trickier.

To fully understand the effectiveness of our retargeting ads or any type of paid ads, we need to understand how our conversions and revenue are being tracked.

There are different ways to determine how much credit to give specific ads determined by how customers interact with ads before purchasing on your website.

This is called attribution models.

In addition to different attribution models, there are click-through conversions and view-through conversions.

Click-through conversions are when a user is shown an ad, clicks on the ad, and then makes a purchase within a certain timeframe – which could be up to 30 days.

A view-through conversions is when a user ONLY is shown an ad, does not click on the ad, but later returns to make a purchase again within a certain timeframe.

With so many options, even once we understand how the tracking works, how, then, do we accurately track which website sales are attributed to our retargeting efforts?

Given the nature of retargeting ads, this can sometimes be difficult to fully answer, but to start, we should look at the different attribution models that Google supports and how to select which attribution model most accurately will track your retargeting conversions.

Google ads currently supports the following five attribution models:

- Last click
- First click
- Linear
- Time decay
- Position-based

Each of these attribution models works a bit differently in tracking conversions for your retargeting ads.

Let us look at these attribution models through a couple of different scenarios where we have the click-through conversion window set at 30 days and the view-through conversion window set at 1 day.

A customer clicks on a Google Shopping ad and does not purchase. A week later, they click on a retargeting ad and DO purchase.

- **Last click** attribution model – 100% credit for the conversion would be attributed to the last click or the retargeting ad. The shopping ad would be given 0% credit.
- **First click** attribution model – 100% credit for the conversion would be attributed to the Google Shopping ad. The retargeting ad would be given 0% credit.
- **Linear** attribution model – With this attribution model, each touchpoint is given equal credit. In our example, both the Google Shopping ad and the Retargeting ad would receive 50% credit for the conversion.
- **Time decay** attribution model – The touchpoint closest to the sale gets most of the credit. In our example, the retargeting ad would get most of the credit while the Google Shopping ad that was clicked on a week before would get very little of the credit.

- **Position-based** attribution model – In this attribution model, 40% of the credit are given to the first and last interaction, and 20% is split between all other touch points. For our example, 40% would be given to the Google Shopping and 40% to the retargeting. Since there were no other touchpoints, then the remaining 20% would be split evenly.

Regardless of which attribution model is being used, in this scenario all except the First click attribution model would appear to accurately account for your retargeting ad's effectiveness.

Note, if you are tracking conversions using first click, then your retargeting ads (if correctly configured) would NEVER show a conversion since you are only serving ads to customers who had previously visited your website.

In this example, a customer clicked on the retargeting ad, and a subsequent conversion occurred. However, what would happen if only seeing the retargeting ads helped facilitate the conversion?

A customer clicks on a Google Shopping ad and does not purchase. A week later, they notice a retargeting ad which reminds them of your product, but they do not click on it. However, 2 days later, the customer returns to the website by typing in the URL and makes a purchase.

- **Last click** attribution model – 100% credit for the conversion would be attributed to the last paid click or the Shopping ad. Unless the view-through conversion window is set at more than 1 day, the retargeting ad would not receive any credit.

- **First click** attribution model – 100% credit for the conversion would be attributed to the first paid click, or in this example, the Shopping ad.
- **Linear** attribution model – With this attribution model, each touchpoint is given equal credit. In our example, both the Google Shopping ad and Direct channel would receive 50% credit for the conversion. The retargeting ad again receives 0% since the view-through conversion window is set at 1 day.
- **Time decay** attribution model – The touchpoint closest to the sale gets most of the credit. In our example, the Direct channel would get most of the credit while the Google Shopping ad that was clicked on a week before would get very little of the credit and retargeting ad again gets 0%.
- **Position-based** attribution model – In this attribution model, 40% of the credit are given to the first and last interaction and 20% is split between all other touch points. For our example, 40% would be given to the Google Shopping and 40% to the Direct channel. Since there were no other touchpoints, then the remaining 20% would be split evenly.

In this scenario, which is fairly common, the retargeting ad would get 0% credit despite being essential in the conversion process. Meanwhile, the Direct channel would receive quite a bit of credit with most of the attribution models despite not being the reason for the sale occurring. This scenario is also what makes tracking retargeting ads difficult when calculating their effectiveness.

Therefore, we need to understand how the attribution models work and then know that the ROAS we calculate for retargeting ads is inevitably going to be a bit lower than reality.

Selecting Your Attribution Model

When you initially configure your conversion tracking, you will define your attribution model as well as your click-through conversion window (the time between click and sale defined as relevant to track conversions) and your view-through conversion window (the time between viewing an ad and not clicking and a sale).

1. Click on Tools & Settings (the wrench icon in the top menu).
2. Click on Conversions below Measurements.
3. Click on the blue plus icon to add a new Conversion Action.
4. You have the option for Website, App, Phone calls or Import. Note that we can only control the attribution model and attribution window through the website option.

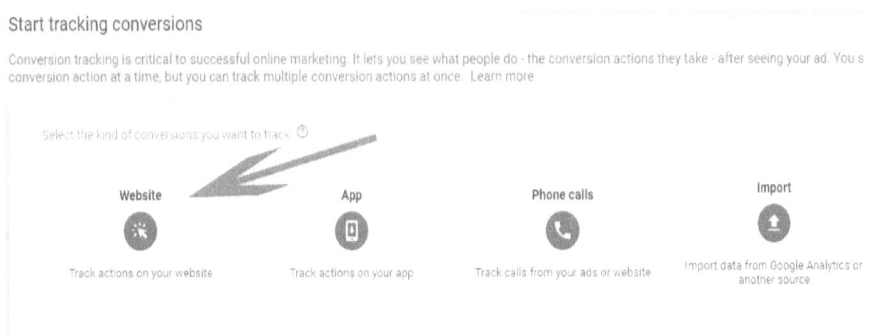

5. Next, you will define the Category you would like to track, name the conversion, how to track the value and how many

6. conversions to count per interaction. Note, for private clients, I recommend the following:

Category – Purchase

Conversion Name – Website Purchase

Value – Use different values for each conversion

Count – Every

7. The next step is how to decide on how to count your conversions. Here, you will define your click-through conversions and view-through conversion window, whether to include in "conversions" and, most importantly, the attribution model.

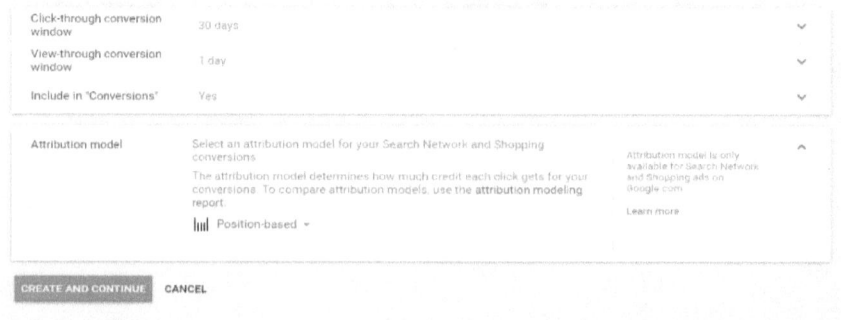

8. Again, what you create for settings will depend on your own preferences, but for private clients, I typically recommend the following:

Click-through conversion window – 30 days.

View-through conversion window – 1 day.

Include in "Conversions" – Yes

Attribution model – Position based

9. Create and Continue. Then follow the instructions Google provides, adding the tag to your website.

Changing The Attribution Model Settings

Even after you have created a conversion action and installed the tracking code, you still have the ability to change the attribution model settings at any time.

To change the attribution model settings, follow these steps:

1. Click on Tools & Settings (the wrench icon in the top menu).
2. Click on Conversions below Measurements.

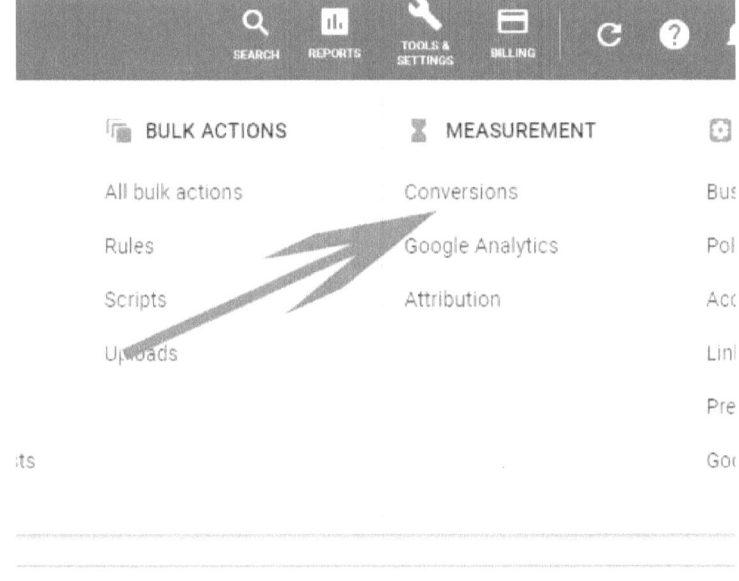

3. Click on existing Conversion action.
4. Click Edit Settings.
5. Change to the desired attribution model, click Save, then DONE.

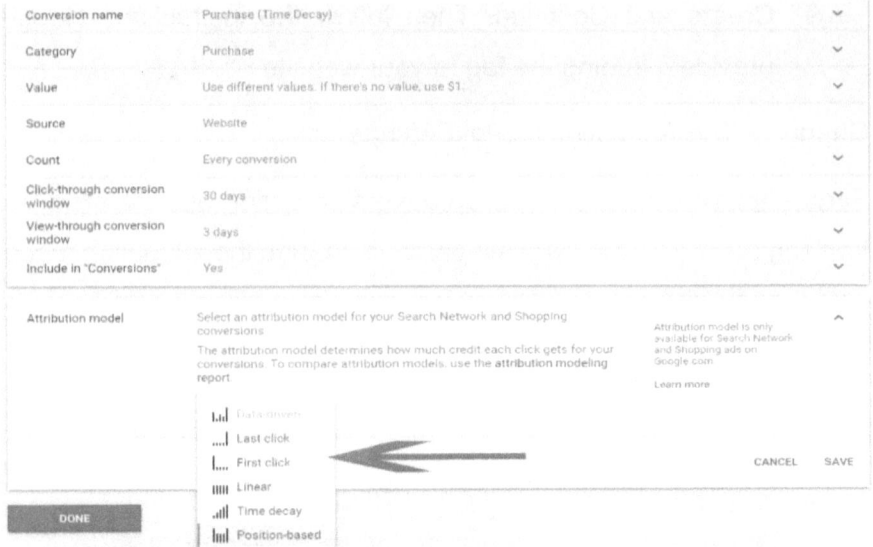

Final Word

Though this chapter, you probably have become aware of the difficulty in properly tracking the full extent of effectiveness with your Google retargeting ads.

Unlike other types of paid ads, due to the nature of retargeting ads, when properly implemented, they are never going to be a stand-alone system of conversion.

Instead, retargeting ads are just a piece of the shopping funnel. They are another touch point that directs those average 97% of customers that initially leave your website without purchasing closer to the ultimate goal of purchasing from your website.

Also, be aware that unless you are bombarding your previous website visitors with an annoying number of ads, retargeting ads are never going to hurt your performance.

Therefore, when calculating your ROAS for your retargeting campaigns, it is important to realize that the profitability typically will be understated.

How much understated?

Well, that all depends on who you ask.

eMarketer has reported that 3 out of every 5 viewers notice and consider ads showing products that they viewed from another page.

Criteo has run a study that shows visitors who are retargeted are 43% more likely to convert than those that are not.

And finally, Word Stream released a study that showed that companies that run retargeting ads show up to 20% more conversions and sales than companies that do not.

The statistics for others are helpful, but not only relevant to your business or your retargeting efforts.

That is why it is essential that you put your own tracking in place to measure and test the effectiveness of different retargeting ads to different audiences.

Because only by tracking to the best of our ability will we be able to increase the effectiveness of our retargeting ads.

Chapter 13

Dotting The I's and Crossing The T's

Before I wrap up this book, I want to share with you one of my favorite stories as it relates to eCommerce store owners.

It is the fable about the Frog and the Scorpion.

The story starts with a Frog sitting by a river and minding his own business when along comes a Scorpion.

The Scorpion walks up to the Frog. "Hello, Mr. Frog," said Scorpion. "I wonder if you might be so kind as to give me a ride across the river on your back."

Now, the Frog knew that the Scorpion could not swim, but still he hesitated. "I don't think that's a good idea," said Frog. "You have a deadly sting, and you might kill me."

"But why would I do that?" replied Scorpion. "If I stung you, we would both die." The Frog thought about what the Scorpion said. "Okay, that makes sense. C'mon Scorpion, jump onto my back, and I will give you a ride across the river," the Frog said.

The Scorpion jumped onto Frog's back, and Frog began to swim across the river. But halfway across, Scorpion took his deadly sting and stuck it into Frog's back.

As the poison shot through the Frog, his body he began to stiffen, and they both began to sink.

"Why?" gasped Frog in his dying breath.

"Sorry, Frog," said Scorpion. "I had to do it, I'm a Scorpion." And Frog and Scorpion both died.

What Is A Small Business Scorpion?

Many small business owners (as frogs) face a scorpion all the time in the form of large Search Engine Marketing (S.E.M.) agencies.

Large S.E.M. agencies face an ongoing issue that is difficult to solve and that most of their clients don't even realize they have.

The larger an agency becomes, the more account executives they need to hire to optimize accounts for their clients. Quite often, the account executives they hire have little to no experience, and most of the time, they are lower-paid positions, either employees right out of college or, many times, overseas employees.

These junior account executives are quickly trained and then let loose to manage accounts, cutting their teeth and learning as they go, all on the client's ad spend. The larger an agency becomes, the more junior marketers they hire, repeating a nasty cycle that typically leads to poor results for their customers.

In addition, possibly even worse than turning over accounts (unbeknown to most clients) to a junior marketer with limited experience, is the fee structure that most search engine marketing companies use to determine what they charge clients.

Typically, clients are charged a percentage of how much they spend on online advertising through the agency. The going rate is between 15 and 20%.

Therefore, junior marketers controlling accounts and the agency they work for are heavily incentivized to spend as much of the client's money as possible, regardless of the results that they are producing.

Avoiding The Scorpion

In order not to be stung by a large S.E.M agency and their team of inexperienced junior marketers that are set to handle your online advertising, you need to arm yourself.

Just like the frog wishes he had carried a stick, if you decide or have already turned over your advertising to a large S.E.M agency, you need to arm yourself with enough knowledge to know whether the S.E.M company you use is following best-practices and if they are spending your advertising budget prudently.

By reading this book, you have taken the first step to avoid being the proverbial frog stung by the scorpion. Below, I will give you some recommendations on where you can go to make sure you are carrying a big stick, at least as it pertains to your knowledge with Google ads.

FINAL WORD

As I finish writing the final chapter for this the newest of the Make Each Click Count book series, the question inevitably will arise: where should you go from here?

Between the covers of the book (you hopefully just read), you will find all tactics and strategies that you need to successfully create and manage a Google retargeting campaign.

Like I guaranteed in the beginning of this book, most likely by the time the book has been published and you have read it, some of the screenshots will probably be outdated (Google likes to move stuff around). However, the strategies and underlying fundamentals provided in this book will continue to perform well when properly applied.

For those of you running a business, you may not have the time to run your own Google Ads campaigns and may end up hiring an agency to run your Google Paid Ads.

That is okay. Many companies don't have the time or resources to manage their Google Ads and still manage to do well in terms of sales and profits.

However, the story I just shared of the of the frog & the scorpion underlie a major problem with completely turning over your online marketing to a large S.E.M (search engine marketing) agency.

That is why you need to make sure you know how to optimize your Google paid ads, and by reading this book, you have taken the first step.

For those of you who can dedicate your time to running your own Google campaigns, congratulations! With the knowledge you have in this book combined with the knowledge of your products, you likely will be able to achieve better results than most agencies using retargeting.

This is great news because after all, who is more concerned about you making a profit than YOU?

Whether you ultimately decide to outsource or to handle Google advertising in-house, I invite you to stay sharp with your marketing in a few ways:

First, check out the other books in this series: *Make Each Click Count Using Google Shopping – Revealing Profits & Strategies* and *Make Each Click Count Using Google Shopping – The T.O.P. Guide To Success Using Google AdWords.* These books offer the same detailed information on running Google Shopping Ads and Google Search Ads. You can find these books available at www.makeeachclickcount.com or on Amazon.

Second, I encourage you to check out my blog at blog.trueonlinepresence.com. Here, you can keep up to date with the latest changes and strategies concerning online advertising and, specifically, Google advertising.

Third, I invite you to check out my private training academy - Make Each Click Count University,

www.makeeachclickcountuniversity.com. Within this site, we offer live training classes that guarantee you will walk away as a bonified expert ready to increase your sales and your profits.

Finally, don't forget to join the private Make Each Click Count Facebook group. It is completely FREE to join. Here, you can interact with myself, other industry experts and immediately join a community of eCommerce professionals.

Regardless of where you go from here, if you are ready to take your online advertising to the next level, I welcome you to join the Make Each Click Count movement and discover what makes us special. Together, we can grow your business!

Happy Marketing!

Andy Splichal

The Make Each Click Count Book Series

Keep In The Know With The Latest In Online Marketing
Make Each Click Count Podcast

Take Your Online Marketing To a Whole New Level With
Make Each Click Count University

Find it all at www.makeeachclickcount.com

www.ingramcontent.com/pod-product-compliance
Lightning Source LLC
Chambersburg PA
CBHW031427210526
45464CB00005B/2087